The
EVERYTHING®
Card Games Book

Dear Reader:

Do you enjoy card games, but find you need clarification on some rules? Have you ever been with a group of friends and wanted to try out a new game? Are you looking to brush up on a card game that you once played? Then this book is for you. Growing up, I absolutely loved playing card games and can remember many evenings spent playing cribbage with my mom. I wrote this book to share my favorite games with you and to give you an introduction to a variety of other solitary games, trick-taking games, gambling games, games for kids, and more. You'll find detailed instructions on how to deal, bid, play, bet, and/or score each game. Since players are constantly changing and adding to the rules, you'll also find known variations of each card game. In many instances I've included a history of the game, and you can even read strategies for winning. So with some friends or by yourself, break out a deck of cards, flip to a game that sounds interesting and learn to play it!

Have Fun and Win Big,

V. M. Katz

The EVERYTHING® Series

Editorial

Publishing Director	Gary M. Krebs
Managing Editor	Kate McBride
Copy Chief	Laura MacLaughlin
Acquisitions Editor	Kate Burgo
Development Editor	Karen Johnson Jacot
Production Editor	Jamie Wielgus

Production

Production Director	Susan Beale
Production Manager	Michelle Roy Kelly
Series Designers	Daria Perreault
	Colleen Cunningham
Cover Design	Paul Beatrice
	Matt LeBlanc
Layout and Graphics	Colleen Cunningham
	Rachael Eiben
	Michelle Roy Kelly
	John Paulhus
	Daria Perreault
	Erin Ring
Series Cover Artist	Barry Littmann

Visit the entire Everything® Series at www.everything.com

THE
EVERYTHING®
CARD GAMES
BOOK

A complete guide to over 50 games
to please any crowd

Nikki Katz

Adams Media
Avon, Massachusetts

To my husband and daughters

Copyright ©2004, F+W Publications, Inc. All rights reserved.
This book, or parts thereof, may not be reproduced
in any form without permission from the publisher; exceptions
are made for brief excerpts used in published reviews.

An Everything® Series Book.
Everything® and everything.com® are registered trademarks of F+W Publications, Inc.

Published by Adams Media, an F+W Publications Company
57 Littlefield Street, Avon, MA 02322 U.S.A.
www.adamsmedia.com

ISBN: 1-59337-130-6
Printed in the United States of America.

J I H G F E D C B A

Library of Congress Cataloging-in-Publication Data
Katz, Nikki.
The everything card games book / Nikki Katz.
p.   cm.
ISBN 1-59337-130-6
1. Card games. I. Title. II. Series: Everything series.

GV1243.K29 2004
795.4–dc22

2004008568

Many of the designations used by manufacturers and sellers to distinguish their products are claimed as trademarks. Where those designations appear in this book and Adams Media was aware of a trademark claim, the designations have been printed with initial capital letters.

This book is available at quantity discounts for bulk purchases.
For information, call 1-800-872-5627.

Contents

Acknowledgments

Thanks to my agent, Barb Doyen, at Doyen Literary Services, Inc., for playing matchmaker and mediator between Adams Media and myself. Another round of applause for my editor, Kate Burgo, for giving me the chance to prove myself with this topic under such short notice.

A loving thank you goes out to my husband, Jason, for dealing with me in times of stress and deadlines. I also want to send my love to my mom, Barb, for all of her support; to my daughters, Katelyn and Kendall, for allowing me to write this book while they were napping; and to my brother, Kenny, for being a great friend. A special thought goes out to my dad, Ken, for always being supportive and wishing the best for me.

Top Ten Places
to Play Cards

1. Play a gambling game at your local casino.

2. Play a game of solitaire on your next plane trip.

3. Play a game against your computer during your next lunch break.

4. Join some friends on the Internet and play a competitive game.

5. Take a trip to Las Vegas or Atlantic City and test your card-game knowledge while seeing the sights.

6. Join a local card group to play your favorite game.

7. Sign up for a card-game tournament and do your best to win.

8. Grab your children and play a family game at your dining-room table.

9. Break out a deck of cards at the next party you attend.

10. Lay out your favorite solitaire game on your bed and relax with some music.

Introduction

▶ ARE YOU SICK OF PLAYING GIN RUMMY but don't know any other card games? Feel like you're going to want to walk out on your spouse if you have an argument over the rules of euchre one more time? Or maybe you're just fed up with expensive, bulky board games that provide no variations? If you answered "Yes!" to any of these questions, then this book is for you. The simple pack of fifty-two cards offers entertainment for players aged eight to eighty, with single-player pastimes like Patience (and the hundreds of variations on the theme) to complex strategy games like Sheepshead. Learning to play card games will give you a sure-fire standby for those rainy days while you're on vacation and offers a far more sociable get-together with friends than watching a movie. Card games are even educational for children, teaching them addition skills, how to match, and all about recognizing suits and numbers.

Almost everybody has a favorite card game and a great mental image of playing cards in the past. Maybe you remember playing War on the floor with your sister, getting angry every time you lost an ace in a battle . . . or maybe you played gin rummy with your grandparents every time they visited to babysit you while your parents went out to dinner . . . or perhaps you played at the blackjack tables with your best friend on spring break in college . . . or maybe you and your husband sat side by side and played video poker on a cruise during your honeymoon. Whatever the game and whatever the source, we all have a favorite card game (or two).

In fact, there are many famous celebrities who have passions for card games. Bill Gates is an avid player of bridge, once playing a twenty-four-hour game with Warren Buffet and their bridge partners. Other bridge fans include Charles Schultz, creator of the *Peanuts* comic strip, and politicians Dwight Eisenhower, Harry Truman, and Chinese premier Deng Xiao Peng. Actors Clint Eastwood, Peter Graves, and Lee Majors were also well-known bridge players. And of course there are a great many celebrity poker players. Ben Affleck, David Schwimmer, Martin Sheen, Mimi Rogers, Carrie Fisher, Hank Azaria, and many others added poker to their card-game resume when playing Celebrity Poker Showdown for their favorite charities on the Bravo television network. Speaking of charities, Dustin Hoffman, James Woods, Kevin Pollack, and Joe Pesci played in a blackjack celebrity fundraiser in Las Vegas in 2002.

But what are the rules for these and other games? Is there a particular strategy that you should follow, or is it all luck of the draw? Are there different ways of playing so that you can add variety to the game when you get bored? *The Everything® Card Games Book* is a great resource to teach you the rules, any history, applicable strategy, possible variations, and everything else you'll need to know about more than 100 card games. If you get stuck on some of the terminology or definitions used, make sure to visit the glossary. Otherwise, it's time to flip to one of these chapters, find a card game that looks interesting, learn the rules, break out a deck of cards, and make some new memories with your family and friends!

Chapter 1

The Evolution of Modern Card Games

What's a good card game without a good deck of cards? The history of card games and playing cards dates back almost 2,000 years to the invention of paper and follows a path from China to the Middle East to Europe and then America. Today's playing cards come cheaply and can be found almost anywhere, but within that deck of fifty-two cards lies a wealth of adventures and culture to be learned.

The First Card Games in Ancient China

T'sai-Lun, from Lei-yang in China, is credited as the inventor of paper circa A.D. 105. Papyrus mats had been used for writing in Egypt for thousands of years, but T'sai-Lun, the chief eunuch of Emperor Ho-Ti, created paper through experimenting with various materials. He finally refined the process and made paper by first grinding plant fibers until they were completely separate and then mixing those fibers with water. The water was strained out of the mixture using a screen, allowing the intertwined fibers to form a flat, thin surface. This thin, flexible, strong paper was known as T'sai Ko-Shi, or "Distinguished T'sai's Paper."

FACT

Some modern card packs used in China still retain the suits of coins and strings of coins (known by mahjong players as "circles" and "bamboos"), and the expression that is used for playing cards means "paper tickets."

The Chinese kept their papermaking secrets to themselves, finally relinquishing the information in the third century to Vietnam and Tibet. In the fourth century, Korea learned the skills, followed by Japan in the sixth century. Somewhere during this time, cards were invented. The first known documentation involving cards is that Emperor Mu-Tsung played domino cards with his wives on New Year's Eve, A.D. 969. These paper dominos were shuffled and dealt just like the modern cards of today. Ancient Chinese "money cards" contained four suits—coins, strings of coins, myriads of strings, and tens of myriads. In fact, these money cards may have actually been currency that was used in gambling games.

The Middle East

Papermaking eventually began traveling west to Baghdad, Damascus, and Cairo as the trade routes carried other goods among the various nations. Of course, cards and card playing followed suit. Around 1400, the Mamelukes of Egypt developed a card deck that is very similar to the deck we play with today. It contained fifty-two cards and had suits of swords, cups, coins, and polo sticks. Each suit consisted of cards numbered one to ten and had three court cards—the king, viceroy, and second under-deputy. The Mameluke court cards did not actually depict people, but they did use the names and represent those particular military officers. The betting game of As-Nas, considered to be a relative of modern poker, was played with five players and a deck of twenty-five cards. Kanjifah is another game that was popular throughout Arabia. Derived from the Indian game Ganjifa, it is played with a circular deck containing eight to twelve suits with ten number and two court cards.

Medieval Europe

Europe was introduced to playing cards in the 1300s, when the new plaything arrived and took the country by storm. There are references to cards in Spain in 1317 and Switzerland in 1377, and by 1380 there were mentions of cards in multiple European cities. These early decks were made up of thin wooden rectangles, decorated with an Arabic style. These cards were created by hand, so they were expensive and often viewed as a status symbol because only the wealthy could afford them. The invention of woodcuts and movable type made it possible to mass-produce the cards, making them easily available and more affordable to the general public. In fact, it is believed that the early card-makers and card-painters at Ulm, Nuremberg, and Augsburg were also wood engravers. Art historians have dated the oldest surviving examples of paper playing cards to the reign of Filippo Maria Visconti, duke of Milan from 1412 to 1447.

ESSENTIAL

For some time, Marco Polo was credited with bringing cards back to Europe following his voyages to China, but the dates do not coincide. Another myth is that soldiers returning from the Crusades brought back decks of playing cards, but the Crusades ended too early for this to be true.

Court Cards

Cards went through a wealth of changes during the 1400s. The court cards were changed to represent European royalty—the king, chevalier, and knave. Queens were introduced in a variety of ways. In some decks, two queens replaced two kings as the highest cards, with the other two kings remaining in the other suits. Other decks contained fifty-six cards, with the four court cards being kings, queens, chevaliers, and knaves. Yet other decks replaced the queens with knights.

The French began naming the court cards after heroes and heroines, especially in the deck of cards made in the manufacturing center of Rouen. In a Rouen deck, the king of spades is David, the king of hearts is Alexander the Great, the king of diamonds is Julius Caesar, and the king of clubs is Charlemagne. The queen of spades is Pallas (also known as Athena), the queen of diamonds is Rachel (mother of Joseph), the queen of clubs is Argine, and the queen of hearts is Judith (of the Apocrypha). The knaves were named after Hector (prince of Troy), La Hire (comrade-in-arms to Joan of Arc), Ogier (a knight of Charlemagne), and Judas Maccabee. The Parisian cards used the same heroes but assigned the kings to different suits. The king of spades is David, the king of hearts is Charlemagne, the king of diamonds is Caesar, and the king of clubs is Alexander.

FACT

The king was always the high card in early card games, but eventually ace-high games were added to the mix. It is believed that the French Revolution introduced ace-high games to represent the lower classes rising above the royalty.

By the late fifteenth century, card decks had become pretty much standard and contained fifty-two cards. The majority of countries dropped the queen, but the French cards replaced their knight with the queen. The lowest court card remained the knave, later changed to the more popular name of jack.

Modern decks of playing cards manufactured in Italy, Spain, Germany, and Switzerland still do not include queens in their court cards. Instead, the third court card is the knight, usually depicted riding a horse.

The Suits

The suits varied across the European countries, but by about 1500 there were three main suit systems that had evolved. The Germanic countries used the suits of hearts, hawk bells, leaves, and acorns. Italian and Spanish cards used the suits of swords, batons (or clubs), coins (or money), and cups (or chalices). French and English cards used the common suits of hearts, spades, diamonds, and clubs.

Laws and Protestations

Because of their popularity and the rising interest in cards, restrictions began to be placed and enforced on both cards and card playing. A German ordinance was introduced in July 1378 that declared specific games punishable by fines if players bet higher than permitted. In France, Edward IV in 1461 and 1462 prohibited playing cards and dice games at any time but the twelve days of Christmas. Henry VII in 1495 and 1496 forbid servants from playing card games except during the twelve days of Christmas, and even then they could play only in their masters' homes.

In Bologna, Italy, in 1423, Cardinal John Capistran, a disciple of Bernadine of Sienna, reportedly organized a massive bonfire of seventy-six sledges, 3,640 backgammon boards, 40,000 dice, and a comparable quantity of cards. Through this time, and despite all the regulations and protestations, cards continued to be manufactured, and card games continued to be played.

Cards Come to America

Cards traveled along with the English to the Americas, possibly arriving with the Puritans on the *Mayflower*. After getting out from underneath English rule, Americans began producing their own playing cards at the beginning of the nineteenth century. They also began adapting their own card games, transforming the French game of Poque into our modern-day version of poker. Casinos were introduced in the early 1800s in New Orleans along the Mississippi River, eventually moving west with the introduction of railroads and the California Gold Rush. Gambling was legalized in 1931 in Nevada, and casinos began sprouting up everywhere to allow players to compete in poker, blackjack, baccarat, and other card games.

The Association of American Card Manufacturers conducted a nationwide study of card playing in November of 1940. The results of that study indicated that cards were the nation's favorite social recreation. As many as 83 percent of the families surveyed played cards, and cards were found in 87 percent of the homes. Families within every income bracket played cards, with rummy being the best-known game: 49 percent of the families surveyed played rummy, followed by solitaire, at 45 percent, and bridge, at 44 percent.

Card games are not as popular today as they once were. With the invention of the television, video games, VCRs, the telephone, and computers, families have many more outlets for game playing. The more popular card games are making a comeback via the computer and the Internet, but the pastime is not nearly as infectious as it was sixty years ago.

A Modern Deck of Cards

Over the years, improvements have been made on the traditional European deck of playing cards. Corner indices were added in the mid-nineteenth century. This enabled players to move their cards closer together and only use one hand during play. Court cards were soon improved to be two-headed and reversible. French court cards once contained full-length images, making it easy for opponents to tell if a player had many court cards—all they had to do was watch to see who turned their cards to view them properly. Cards were eventually varnished on the surface to add to their longevity and allow them to take wear. The square corners were eventually replaced with rounded corners, preventing bends and dog-eared cards.

The standard card today measures about 2½ inches by 3½ inches (6 cm by 9 cm). The backs are printed with identical designs, patterns, or pictures. A full deck is printed on pasteboard made up of two sheets gummed together with black paste to ensure opaqueness.

ALERT!

Dirty cards can leave a mark on your game by showing which cards you hold. Clean your deck with cold water and a soft cloth. Then dry them immediately with another soft cloth, and spread them out on a table to dry. Never place your cards near a heat source!

The Suits

Cards manufactured in the United States use the French suits of clubs ♣, diamonds ♦, spades ♠, and hearts ♥. The four suits are said to represent the structure of medieval society. The clubs represent agriculture, diamonds represent the merchant class, spades represent the military, and the hearts represent the church. Each suit contains thirteen cards. They are ranked, from highest to lowest as ace, king, queen, jack, ten, nine, eight, seven, six, five, four, three, and two.

The Jokers

Modern decks today come with fifty-two cards within the four suits and two nonsuited cards, the jokers. Around 1870 in the United States, the game of euchre introduced the joker as the "best bower" and the highest-ranking trump card over the jacks as left and right bowers. Euchre was often referred to as "Juker" (a German term for "jack"), and so the joker card might be a play on the term "Juker card." By the 1880s, the joker card was illustrated as a clown or a jester, and this is how we see jokers in play today.

Tarot Cards

During the first half of the 1400s (probably between 1420 and 1440), the first set of tarot cards was created in northern Italy. The set was very similar to standard playing card decks in that it included four suits of number cards from one to ten and three court cards in each suit of a page, a knight, and a king. The tarot deck also included a queen in each suit, which was added to the court cards, and twenty-two "special" cards that did not belong to a suit. These symbolic werecards were named to be typically distinctive to European Christendom and included the Pope, Death, the Empress, the Devil, Angel, Sun, Moon, World, Traitor, Justice, and more.

The tarot card pack was used to play a new card game, similar to bridge, where twenty-one of the special cards served as permanent trumps. These trump cards could be played regardless of the suit led and they outranked any number or court cards. This "Game of Triumphs" became extremely popular among the elite upper classes and spread throughout Europe.

FACT

The Fool card could be played at any time, regardless of whether the player held a card in the suit led or any trump cards. The Fool card could not win a trick and was played so you did not have to lose a different card. If you played the Fool, you kept the card and handed a previously won card to the winner of that trick, as a replacement.

As the tarot trump cards entered new countries, changes were made to the pictures on the special cards to pertain to that country's beliefs, spirituality, and culture. The ranking of the trumps also changed, as they did not contain any numbers. In its course of travel, the pack was extended to ninety-seven cards by adding more trumps; shortened to sixty-three cards by removing lower-value numeric cards; converted to use the French suits; and shortened to fifty-four cards by dropping numeric cards. No matter what the changes, the deck was always used to play trick-taking games.

Hundreds of years later, devotees of the occult arts in France and England saw mystical and enchanting meanings in the symbols of the tarot cards. Their fascination and use of the cards turned into the present-day view that we have of tarot cards as a deck of mystic and divine cards used in fortune-telling and the occult.

Today, the tarot deck contains seventy-eight cards, broken up into the major arcana and the minor arcana. The twenty-two special cards make up the major arcana and are said to represent various aspects of a person's life and the world. The fifty-six cards (the standard fifty-two cards plus the four pages) that make up the minor arcana contain the four suits of wands, pentacles, swords, and cups that are said to represent various life stages, the four elements, times of day, seasons, and different powers.

Card Games on the Big and Small Screen

Although not as popular today as they were in the early and mid-1900s, cards and their games have infiltrated our culture and are seen in all aspects of life. The king and queen of hearts have both made it big on the music charts, and who hasn't seen the artwork of dogs playing poker? Of course, the biggest arena for showcasing card-game strategy and talent is on the big and small screen. Many television shows and movies, some well known and some often unheard of, have included or have been centered on card games:

- *ANGELS OVER BROADWAY* (1940)—Hustler Bill O'Brian tries to entice Charles Engle, an embezzler with a suicide note, to play a card game so he can relieve him of his money.
- *MAVERICK* (1957)—Brothers Bret and Bart Maverick migrate from town to town as they travel across the West, playing five-card draw or other poker variations.
- *THE CINCINNATI KID* (1965)—An up-and-coming poker-playing Steve McQueen tries to prove himself in a high-stakes match against "the Man," a master of the game.
- *A BIG HAND FOR THE LITTLE LADY* (1966)—It's time for Joanne Woodward to save the day, and her family's savings, when her husband collapses on the floor in the middle of a poker hand.
- *KALEIDOSCOPE* (1966)—Warren Beatty is the ultimate gambler when he marks high-value cards so that he can cheat in a game of no-limit blackjack.
- *PLAY CARDS!* (1968)—A game show structured around five-card poker hands. Two contestants and a celebrity competed against one another to build the best hand.

- ***GAMBIT* (1972)**—Host Wink Martindale pitted married contestants against one another while playing a large-card variation of blackjack as they answered questions and attempted not to take cards that would push their hands over twenty-one points.

- ***THE JOKER'S WILD* (1972)**—Although this game show was not based on a card show, host Jack Barry did employ the joker as a wild card, which could mean an automatic win if a contestant spun a triple joker and answered a question correctly.

- ***CALIFORNIA SPLIT* (1974)**—This is one of a few movies that attempts to show the day-to-day life of card-playing, sports-betting, sleep-till-noon gamblers.

- ***CARD SHARKS* (1978)**—This game show had contestants pitting card-game knowledge against one another in a version of Acey-Deucey. A base card was turned up, and the player had to guess whether the next card would be higher or lower than that card. The first player to make it through five cards, answering questions along the way, went to the final round for big money.

- ***HONEYMOON IN VEGAS* (1992)**—Nicholas Cage loses more than he gambled when he has to clear a poker debt by giving his fiancée up for the weekend!

- ***HOUSE OF GAMES* (1997)**—In David Mamet's directorial film debut, psychologist Lindsay Crouse discovers that her patient, Joe Mantegna, owes a $25,000 gambling debt and becomes involved on behalf of her patient.

- ***THE JAMES BOND MOVIES* (1962 ON)**—In many of the James Bond movies and books, Agent 007 enjoys a game of baccarat at the world's most luxurious casinos. And like his luck with the ladies, James Bond seems to have a way with the cards.

- ***ROUNDERS* (1998)**—After Matt Damon loses his tuition money in a high-stakes poker game, he vows to give up gambling. Unfortunately, his friend Edward Norton shows up and needs a bit of help with some unpaid debts.

Now that you know a little about the history of cards, let's move on to what you need to know to get started playing!

Chapter 2

The Basics

If you're new to playing card games, there is some basic information that you should know. You'll want the best seat available, depending on what the game is and who is playing, and when it's your turn to deal you'll need to be able shuffle the cards and deal them out accordingly. If you're playing a game that involves gambling, you need to know about betting, and it's always good to know when to fold your cards in a game of poker!

Claiming Your Seat at the Card Table

There are various strategies for sitting at a card table, as well as different layouts and requirements for seating. Some card games require that you and your opponents cut the cards to determine your seats. The player who cuts the highest card (kings are high and aces are low) chooses her seat. The player who cut the second-highest card chooses his seat next, and so on. In partnership games, a player and his partner sit across from one another at the table. If seating positions are going to be chosen by cutting the cards, the player who takes the highest card essentially chooses the seats for everyone because he takes his seat, his partner sits across from him, and their opponents sit in the remaining two seats.

If you know your opponents, you can strategize where you would like to sit at the table based on whom you would like to sit next to. If you know that another player does not count cards or pay close attention to the game, you will want to sit to the left of that player (in a card game that is played clockwise) in order to take advantage of that player's discards.

Blackjack Seating

In the game of blackjack, there are different strategies to employ before claiming a seat. If you use a card-counting system, you will want to sit to the far left of the table (often called "third base") so you can see more cards before playing your hand. If the dealer is bad at concealing his cards, you will want to sit in whatever position is best to see the hole card (the first card that the dealer deals himself, face down). It is a misconception that sitting at third base can affect the dealer's hand. Many players feel that if you sit at third base and hit when you shouldn't, taking a card that would have made the dealer bust, or you don't hit when you should and the dealer gets a card that helps his hand, that your play was responsible for helping or ruining the dealer's hand. In actuality, as long as the cards are shuffled enough to be randomized, improper play will help the other players as often as it hurts them.

When playing at a blackjack table, the seat closest to the dealer that gets dealt to first is known as first base. The seat closest to the dealer that gets dealt to last, before the dealer, is known as third base.

Poker Seating

When playing poker, experts feel that choosing a seat at the table is very important—a detail the beginning player often overlooks. If you sit to the dealer's right (or in the position that is dealt last), you are also the player to bet last. This gives you an opportunity to analyze and evaluate the other players' hands. In general, you want loose and aggressive players on your right side, acting before you in most hands. That way, you know whether they plan to raise when you decide what you want to do, and you can call a bet with more marginal cards with less fear of being raised. You want tight and passive players on your left. You do not fear a raise from them, and you can often raise and cause them to fold their cards.

Shuffling the Cards

A shuffle is the randomization of a deck of cards by "interleaving" the cards multiple times. You shuffle the cards by dividing the cards up into two nearly equal stacks and placing them into both hands. You then alternately interleave the cards from your left and right hands to combine the two stacks together. Some people do this by flapping the cards down using their fingers and thumbs, while others just push the stacks together.

Shuffling a deck by exactly interleaving the two halves of a deck is called a riffle shuffle. Shuffling a deck by placing cards in randomly chosen positions is known as an exchange shuffle.

Types of Shuffles

The riffle shuffle is modeled by cutting the deck exactly in half and dropping cards one by one from each hand. In 1992, David Bayer and Persi Diaconis proved that after seven random riffle shuffles of a deck with fifty-two cards, every configuration of the cards is nearly equally likely. A deck shuffled fewer than six times shows a similarity to the original deck, but shuffling more than seven times does not increase the randomness of the shuffle.

Scientifically, there exists an in-shuffle, where the two stacks are interleaved from the left hand first, and an out-shuffle, where the two stacks are interleaved from the right hand first. If you had a deck with only six cards (1 2 3 4 5 6), the in-shuffle would result in a new deck of 4 1 5 2 6 3, and the out-shuffle would result in a new deck of 1 4 2 5 3 6.

How Many Arrangements?

If you play games often, you've probably shuffled a deck of cards, or even multiple decks of cards, hundreds of times. But do you know just how many different arrangements those fifty-two cards could create? You'll probably be surprised at the answer.

To demonstrate how to calculate the number of possible arrangements, imagine that you have fifty-two choices for picking out the first card, fifty-one choices for picking out the second card (since one card has already been pulled out of the deck), and so on. This continues on until there is only one selection remaining to pull out of the deck. So the possible number of arrangements in a deck is obtained by multiplying 52 x 51 x 50 ... and so on to 2 x 1. In mathematics this is referred to as 52! (or "52 factorial"). Shockingly enough, the expression 52! is a sixty-eight digit number: 80,658,175,170,943,878,571,660,636,856,403,766,975,289,505, 440,883,277,824,000,000,000,000.

In essence, this means that it is practically impossible for you to shuffle the deck in the same arrangement twice in your lifetime.

Cutting the Deck

In most card games, after the dealer is done shuffling the cards, the player to his right or left will cut the cards. In order to cut the deck, you will remove as one unit roughly half of the cards from the top of the deck, placing that part of the deck on the table next to the remaining cards. The dealer then picks up the bottom half of the deck, places it on top of the other stack, and squares the deck. The purpose of cutting the cards is to vary who gets a specific hand after they are dealt. Let's assume that a game includes four players and the entire deck is going to be dealt out. If you cut the cards at card twenty-one, the hands will be shifted by one player (divide twenty-one by four and there is one card left over).

QUESTION?

Can I shuffle by cutting the cards?
No. Repeatedly cutting cards is not the same as shuffling a deck. Repeated cutting is the same as cutting once in a different place because the order of the cards is not being changed.

Some card games use a method of cutting the deck to determine who the first dealer will be. In this case, you each cut a small unit of the deck and look at the bottom card of the portion that you hold. This number determines whether you will or will not be the first dealer. Kings are high and aces low when cutting cards. If two or more players cut the same card, they may either cut again or randomly select a card from the stack.

Betting and Checking

In all of the poker games as well as blackjack, Red Dog, and baccarat, you will be placing bets on your hand in the hopes of winning money from the bank or your opponents. In games such as Pai Gow poker, blackjack, baccarat, and Red Dog, you will place an initial bet on the table. This bet must fall between a minimum and maximum bet that is documented on the casino table or that you have all agreed on when you play at home. In these games, your bet will typically remain the same throughout the hand. In a few instances you can increase your bet by doubling down (doubling your bet to receive one and only one more card to add to your hand) or splitting a pair (doubling your bet to split a pair of cards into two separate hands to play) in blackjack, or you can raise your bet in Red Dog. After you have played out your hand, you will win or lose your bet based on a comparison between your hand and the dealer's hand. You will lose your bet if your hand loses to the dealer's hand. You will push your bet if your hand ties the dealer's hand, meaning that you get back your original bet and win/lose nothing. You can win money if your hand beats the dealer's hand.

ALERT!

If you play the games of baccarat or Pai Gow poker in a casino, they will take a small commission out of your winnings. This amount is usually 5 percent, or less, of the amount that you win and helps the casino maintain its edge on the players.

Betting limits are typically expressed with a minimum and maximum (for instance, $5–$10) and may be spread-limit or structured-limit. In a spread-limit game, you may bet any dollar amount between the minimum and maximum bet. When you want to raise the bet, it must also be within the minimum and maximum range. In a structured-limit game, you may only bet and raise the minimum dollar amount during the first few rounds of play, and the maximum dollar amount during the last few rounds of play.

The Dealer

The dealer is the person who deals out the cards during a specific round or hand of play. There are two types of dealers—dealers in home games or in a card group who are also players in the game, and dealers in a casino.

When the players are also the dealers, the first dealer is usually chosen at random or by cutting the cards. In most instances, all of the players take turns dealing, and after the first hand, the deal typically passes to the player on the left. In many card games, players will play with two decks, each with a different back. While one player is dealing, the next player will shuffle the deck of cards just played and place it to the right of the next dealer. This saves time, allowing more hands and games to be enjoyed.

In a casino, the dealer is an employee who staffs the games in the casino. He goes through extensive training to learn how to correctly shuffle the cards, deal the cards, and pay out money to the casino players. The players will never get to deal the cards, as it would leave room for error and cheating. In blackjack, the players play against the dealer, so he deals himself a hand. In poker, the dealer is not a participant; instead, the players play against each other, so the dealer does not deal himself a hand. (An exception to this is in Pai Gow poker, where the players do not play against one another but against the dealer, as in blackjack.)

Dealing the Cards

Each card game has its own requirements for dealing out the cards, and you need to know them when it's your turn to deal. You must first know the order that the cards should be dealt out to each player (clockwise, counterclockwise, or another varied pattern). The majority of card games are dealt clockwise. The next step to learning how to deal is to know if the cards are dealt face down or face up. In some games, all cards are dealt face down. Other times, the last card will be turned up to determine the trump suit (a suit that wins over the other three suits). The dealer then picks up that card after the first trick is played. In other games, some of the cards are dealt face down while others are dealt face up. As you learn the rules for a new game, pay close attention to whether the cards are dealt face up or down.

You must also know how many cards are dealt out at a time. The majority of card games require cards to be dealt one at a time, but in some games the cards are dealt out in groups of two, three, or more cards. To complete the deal, you must know the total of how many cards are dealt out to each player. Every card game varies in the amount of cards dealt in a hand. In cribbage, only six cards are dealt to each player, while each player in spades gets thirteen.

After dealing out the cards, you must know what should be done with the remainder of the deck. If the card game does not require that the deck be completely dealt out, something must be done with the remaining cards. Sometimes they will form a stockpile and a discard pile that players will draw from during play. Other games require a kitty, or side area, that a player or multiple players will add to their hand at a later point in the game. In a variety of games, the cards are just placed to the side of the dealer and never viewed in the hand.

FACT

Employees of casinos have specific methods for dealing cards that they all follow, every time. For instance, in dealing blackjack cards from a shoe (a dealing device), a dealer removes the card with his left index finger, slides the card to his right hand while turning it over, and places the card lightly down on the table as if pointing to the player's spot with the card.

As the dealer, you also need to know if there is a discard-and-replace step in the game. In a few card games, the players are allowed to discard cards from their hand, which are replaced by the dealer from the cards remaining in the deck. These cards are not dealt one at a time. Instead, they are dealt in a group to the player before moving to the next player who discards. Some gambling card-games also have cards that are dealt out at a later point in the game. There are usually rounds of betting in between, and then another card is dealt to each player or to a communal area on the table.

As the dealer, you must know all of these requirements before it's your turn to deal. You need to either follow them, suffer the need to re-deal, or pass your deal on to the next player.

Etiquette

Proper etiquette is important when playing cards, especially in a casino, in tournaments, or when playing older, well-established card games. Some standard rules of etiquette apply to all games and should typically be adhered to.

Etiquette in Dealing

When being dealt to, you should pick up your cards after the last card is dealt, not each time you receive a card. If you're the dealer, you should never attempt to view the bottom card while dealing, even if it is dealt to you as the last player. If you're the first player to play your turn, you should wait until all players have organized their hands and appear ready to play.

Etiquette During Play

While playing the game, there should be minimal conversation and it should be applicable to the game itself. In between games, or when the hands are being shuffled and dealt, conversation is appropriate. If a game involves bidding or betting, you should make the statements clearly and loud enough for the entire table to hear. You should not hesitate in your bid or bet, or use an inflection or special emphasis, as this may be considered a signal and is not allowed.

Novelty decks of cards with artistic renditions on the backs are frowned upon during a serious game. A new deck of cards, or one without marks and dog-eared corners, is necessary to prevent identification of cards during play.

It is improper to praise or critique or criticize yourself or your opponents during play. This means you should also not draw attention to your score or your opponent's score. In a trick-taking game, you should not call attention to the number of tricks needed to complete or defeat a bid.

You should not detach a card from your hand before it's your turn to play, and if you know that you are going to win a trick, you should never prepare to gather the cards before all four players have played. If a player folds his hand or wins a hand, you should not ask or insist upon seeing that hand unless the rules specify that the hand be displayed.

Following social etiquette is the best way to have fun, play a great game of cards, and allow others to enjoy their time as well. You don't want to play a game that involves cheating, signals, loud talking, or obnoxious players. That defeats the purpose of getting together to play!

Chapter 3

E Card Games for One Player

One-player card games are a great way to pass the time when you're stuck on a long flight or looking for a way to pass the afternoon. With more than a thousand variations of about twelve base games, solitaire games help get your brain working and can keep you occupied for hours at a time. One-player card games are now also available on any personal computer and on many cell phones!

Solitaire/Patience/Klondike

Although it is often referred to as solitaire, the name of this game is actually Klondike. In most of Europe it is referred to as Patience, and in Spain it is called *Solitario.* Klondike is an easy-to-play, extremely well-known card game that is part chance and part strategy. It is also one of the most difficult games to win! The objective of Klondike is to fill up the suit stacks, each stack containing one suit in sequence, from ace to king.

Setup of Klondike

Klondike uses the standard deck of fifty-two cards. There are three areas to the playing field that you will be using. The area across the top of the playing field is where you'll place your building stacks. Building stacks are the cards on the table that you will be playing with, moving single cards and groups of cards within these stacks and placing the cards on top of one another if they are available.

In Klondike, seven building stacks are dealt out horizontally. The first stack on the left has one card facing up. The second stack has one card face down and the top card is face up. The third stack has two cards face down and the top card is face up, and so on, until the seventh stack has six cards face down and the top card is face up. The remainder of the cards are placed face down in a stockpile, located in the upper left corner of the playing field (above the building stacks), with a waste pile below it. The stockpile allows you to continue the game when you are unable to move anymore cards within the building stacks. The waste pile is used for cards that are turned over from the stockpile that you are unable to use. The card on top of the waste pile is available for play, but the cards beneath that are unavailable for play until you first use the cards above.

You'll want to leave a third area for the suit stacks, which will be four stacks of cards in the upper right-hand corner of the playing field. Filling up the suit stacks is the goal of the game. You'll be building each stack from ace to king in one suit. If you can get all of your cards into those suit stacks, you win!

Rules of Play

In playing Klondike (and almost all solitaire games), you move cards and sequences of cards around the playing field, and you need to be constantly on the lookout for an available play. If you have an ace that is showing, and as aces show during play, they should be immediately moved to an open suit stack. You can add to the suit stack with the next sequential value in that same suit (for instance, you can place a 2♥ on an A♥).

Within the building stacks, a card may only be moved onto another card if it is of the opposite color and if the card it is being placed on is of a value one higher—for instance, you can place a Q♥ on a K♠. You can move multiple cards onto another card as long as they are in a sequence and the top card is being moved to a card that is of opposite color and next higher value. That is, you can move a sequence of 7♣ 8♥ 9♠ onto a 10♥ or 10♦). A king has the highest value and may not be placed on any other number. If you clear the top card (facing up) from a stack by moving it to another stack or by moving it to a suit stack, you may turn over the next card in the pile that is facing down. If you clear all the cards in a stack, you may move any king into that empty space. If you can no longer move any cards, you may turn over the first three cards from your stockpile onto your waste pile, but only the top card is available for play. If it does not play, or when you can no longer move any more cards, you may turn over another three cards from the stockpile onto the waste pile. When you're out of cards in the stockpile, turn over the waste pile and move it back up to become the stockpile again, and continue drawing cards in sets of three as needed.

Build your stacks evenly, and try not to let any one sequence get too far ahead of the others. Play any available cards from the stacks before using cards from the waste pile. If you have a choice between two top cards, choose the one that has a deeper stack.

Strategy is a factor in the game of Klondike when you have multiple choices of moves. For example, you might have a 7♦ open and the option to move a 6♣ from the waste pile or a 6♠ from a building stack. If you move the 6♣ from the waste pile, you might be opening up more cards within the waste pile that will help you later. But if you move the 6♠ from a building stack, you might be opening up more cards within that stack. You won't know if your move was the right one until the game ends—either with all fifty-two cards in the suit stacks, or when no further cards may be moved.

Variations

There are a couple different variations of Klondike. In Las Vegas Klondike, cards from the stockpile are turned up one at a time, and you only go through the stockpile once. If you play it as a gambling game, you pay $50 to the dealer for a hand, and you win $5 for each card that you are able to play to a suit stack. In Joker Solitaire, two jokers are added to the deck, one designated as a black joker and one as a red joker. When the black joker is turned up, it may be used as any black card as long as both black cards of that value are not visible or have been played to the suit stacks. The same rules apply to the red joker.

Free Cell

Free Cell is a strategic solitaire game that gives you the use of four free locations to place troublesome cards. Almost every deal can be solved, with a few exceptions. The objective of Free Cell is to move all fifty-two cards into the suit stacks, each stack with one suit from ace to king.

Setup of Free Cell

Free Cell uses a standard pack of fifty-two cards. You use three areas of the playing field. The area across the bottom of the playing field is where you'll deal out eight building stacks horizontally. The first four stacks will have eight rows of face-up cards, and the second four stacks will have seven rows of face-up cards. Place each row of cards slightly overlapping the previous row so all cards are visible, the last cards in each row being the ones that can be played. Leave an area for four cards in the upper left-hand corner of the playing field, above your building stacks. These will be a temporary storage for cards and are called the "free cells." Also leave an area for your suit stacks in the upper right-hand corner of the playing field, to be added to as the game progresses. The first card to be laid down must be an ace, followed by a two, three, four, and so on until the king is the final card to be added to the suit stack. Once all cards are in their individual suit stacks in this order, the game is complete.

Rules of Play

Like Klondike, Free Cell involves moving around a lot of cards within the building stacks. A card may only be moved onto another card within the building stacks if it is of the opposite color and if the card it is being placed on is of the next value (for instance, you can place a 3♥ on a 4♣). You can move a group of cards onto another card as long as they are in a sequence and you will continue the sequence by making the move. A king has the highest value and may not be placed on any other card. An ace may be moved to an empty suit stack and added to by placing the next value of the same suit on that card. If you clear all the cards of a building stack by placing them on other building stacks or moving them to the suit stacks, you may move any one card into that free space.

Try to leave the cells open, as this allows more cards to be moved at a time. Try building on kings as soon as you can, and make sure that kings are not covering other cards, because they cannot be built upon. Build your sequences evenly.

If you can no longer move any cards, you may place any available card in one of the empty free cells, bringing it back into play when you can place it on a suit stack or on a card in the playing field of opposite color and one value higher. There can only be one card in a free cell at a time, and you will be moving cards in and out of these cells to maximize your playing potential. The game ends when all fifty-two cards are in the suit stacks or when no further cards may be moved.

Golf

If it's a rainy day and you can't hit the golf course, why not play a round of golf at home? In this solitaire game, your objective is to place all of the cards from your playing field into the waste pile. This makes it different than the majority of solitaire games in which your goal is to place all of the cards in suit stacks.

Setup of Golf

Golf uses a standard deck of fifty-two cards. There are two areas of the playing field. The area across the top of the playing field is where you'll place your building stacks. These seven stacks of five face-up cards are dealt horizontally. Each card is visible and overlaps the card above it so that all the cards can be seen, but only the bottom card can be played. The remaining seventeen cards are placed face down in a stockpile located in the lower left corner of the playing field (below the building stacks), with a waste pile to the right of it. The top card of the stockpile is placed face up to become the waste pile.

Rules of Play

In the game of Golf, you do not move cards within the building stacks. Instead you move them to the waste pile. You start by moving any free card from the building stacks to the waste pile. A free card is one that is not covered by another card. If any free card in the building stacks is one value higher or lower than the top card of the waste pile, move that free card to the top of the waste pile. The colors and suits of the card do not matter (so that you can place a 7♥ on a 6♦ or 8♠). Continue moving free cards to the waste pile until you can no longer move any cards. You now will turn over the next card in your stockpile and place it on top of the waste pile. You then search your playing field for cards that are one value higher or lower than the new card turned up.

The game ends when all of your cards from the playing field are in the waste pile or when no further cards may be moved. Variations of Golf include wrapping (a king may be played on an ace and vice versa), no wrapping (a king may not be played on an ace or vice versa), and setting a time limit for the game. If you do not finish the game in the time allotted, the game is automatically over.

La Belle Lucie

La Belle Lucie, also known as the Fan, is a fun solitaire game with multiple stacks. The objective of La Belle Lucie is to fill up the suit stacks by building them with available cards, with each stack containing one suit built up in the sequence ace to king, using a standard deck of fifty-two cards. There are two areas to the playing field. Deal seventeen building stacks, each with three cards face up in a fan style with one card available and overlapping the other two cards. The last remaining card in the deck is placed as its own fan. You also leave an area for the suit stacks, which will be four stacks of cards in the upper right-hand corner of the playing field, above the building stacks.

FACT

Most solitaire games can be played within a small space on your tabletop. Some of the games do require a larger space, but they can be played on the floor or on top of your bed, or you can invest in a deck of miniature playing cards to use less space.

Rules of Play

A card is only available if it is not partially covered by another card, so at the beginning of play only the ends of the fans are available. An ace should be moved immediately to the suit stack and can be added to by placing a two of the same suit on that card, followed by a three, four, and so on until the suit stack is complete from ace to king. If a card cannot be moved to a suit stack, it can be moved to the end of another fan if the available card on that fan is of a higher value of the same suit. As an example, if the 3♥ is available at the end of one fan, it may be moved to the 4♥ if available on another fan. Once you have moved the 3♥ onto the 4♥, the second card underneath the 3♥ in the first fan is now uncovered and may be played. The 4♥ is now unavailable because it is covered by the 3♥.

Redealing the Playing Field

When all possible moves have been played, with cards going to the suit stacks and on top of other fans, you should gather up all of the remaining fans. You'll then shuffle the cards and re-deal them in fans of three, with any one or two remaining cards becoming a fan of their own. Only two re-deals are allowed—if you've re-dealt twice and can move no more cards, the game is over. You win when all fifty-two cards are in the suit stacks.

The Game of Montana

Montana is a relatively new game of solitaire that is also known by the names Gaps and Blue Moon. The goal is simple, but execution can be quite difficult. The objective of Montana is to rearrange the cards in four rows in ascending order, from two to king, using a standard deck of fifty-two cards. Start out by dealing all fifty-two cards in four rows of thirteen cards each. All cards should be dealt face up, and they should not overlap one another, making all cards available for play. Then remove the four aces to create four "holes" within the playing area.

You'll start playing by moving a card from any position on the playing area to one of the holes as long as that card is one value higher than, and the same suit as, the card to the left. For instance, you can place a 6♣ to the right of a 5♣. Only a two may be placed at the beginning of the row (to the left), and no cards can be placed to the right of a king. If no further cards can be moved, you'll pick up all unordered cards from each row and shuffle them with the aces. Re-deal the cards into the empty spaces in the rows, and remove the four aces again. Play continues as before. Three re-deals are allowed before declaring the game over. The game ends when all fifty-two cards form four rows in ascending order or when no more plays are available.

The Game of Monte Carlo

Monte Carlo is an advanced matching game that requires you to think ahead and strategize the future movement of your cards once others have been placed in the discard pile. The objective of Monte Carlo is to place all fifty-two cards in the discard pile. There are three areas of the playing field. The "table" is created by dealing out five columns of five cards each, without any cards overlapping. You'll want to leave an area for a discard pile on the right side of the playing field. Pairs of cards with the same value will be placed here. The remaining twenty-seven cards are placed face down on the right side of the playing field, below the discard pile, to create the stockpile.

FACT

Lady Adelaide Cadogan is thought to have written the first book on the rules of solitaire and patience games, just after the Civil War. In fact, in England, "Cadogan" is a household name for solitaire.

To play Monte Carlo, discard pairs of cards of the same rank (for example, discard a 10♠ and a 10♥) that are adjacent to each other, whether horizontally, vertically, or diagonally—that is, any two cards that touch top to bottom, side to side, or diagonally at the corners. When there are no available pairs of cards to remove, move all of the cards left to fill up blank spaces. Then wrap the first card in a row to the end of the row above so that each of the top rows contains five cards. When you are done, use cards from the stockpile to complete the grid. The game ends when all fifty-two cards are in the discard pile or when no further cards may be moved.

The Game of Pyramid

You won't be traveling to Egypt to play this solitary card game. Pyramid is a game of addition, and it requires you to strategize the sequence in which you pick up your cards. The objective of Pyramid is to place all fifty-two cards in the discard pile by moving pairs of cards totaling thirteen, or a single king with a value of thirteen, to the pile. There are three areas of the playing field. The area in the middle of the playing field is where you'll place your pyramid. Deal the pyramid with twenty-eight cards arranged in seven rows face up. The top row has one card. The second row has two cards, placed partially over the first row. The third row has three cards, also placed partially over the second row, and so on until the seventh row has seven cards, placed partially over the sixth row. You'll place the remaining twenty-four cards face up in a stockpile located in the upper left corner of the playing field with the waste pile below it. The first card on top of the stockpile is turned face up and is available, and as soon as any cards are placed in the waste pile, the top card there is available for play as well. You'll want to leave an area for the discard pile on the right side of the field.

Study the pyramid to make sure the game can be won. Make sure that each card has enough matches to free it without the two matching cards blocking each other. If possible, use a match from the waste pile.

You cannot remove a card from the pyramid if it is covered by another card. Two cards must be removed to unlock a card in the upper rows in the middle of the pyramid, but the cards on the sides of the pyramid only need one removal to become available.

If there is a king available, you may move it to the discard pile. If there are two cards available within the pyramid, or one card that can be combined with the top card on the waste pile or stockpile to make thirteen, you may move both of those cards to the discard pile. The jack is worth eleven, and the queen is worth twelve for making pairs with ones and twos. If there are no more cards able to be moved, you may take the top card from the stockpile, place it on the waste pile, and attempt to use the next stockpile card to create a pair to be removed. One variation of Pyramid is to remove three cards from the stockpile and attempt to make pairs using any of the three cards in play with the pyramid. The game ends when all fifty-two cards are in the discard pile or when no further pairs can be created.

Spider

Spider solitaire is a very popular solitaire card game and is often called the "king of all solitaires." Along with Free Cell, Spider was made popular when it was introduced as a standard game in the Windows operating system from Microsoft. It's quite addictive to play. The object of Spider is to build eight suit sequences from king to ace. Unlike most solitaire games, these cards are not moved to suit stacks. Instead, the sequences are built in descending order within the building stacks in the playing field.

Setup of Spider

Spider uses two standard decks of fifty-two cards. There are two areas of the playing field. The area across the top of the playing field is where you'll place your building stacks. Ten stacks are dealt horizontally, filling this area. The first four stacks have six cards each, with the top card facing up and the other five cards facing down. The remaining six stacks have five cards each, with the top card facing up and the other four cards facing down. You'll place the remainder of the cards face down to form a stockpile.

Rules of Play

A card may only be moved onto another if the card it is being placed on is of the next value—the suit and color do not matter. (In other words, you can place a queen on any king.) You can move multiple cards onto another card as long as they are in a sequence and in the same suit and as long as the top card is being moved to a card that is of the next higher value. A king has the highest value and may not be placed on any other number.

Try to get as many open stacks as possible and build your sequences in their proper suits, even if it means juggling cards around the board. Forming a thirteen-card sequence as soon as possible will also help by clearing cards off the playing area.

If you clear the top card (facing up) from a building stack, you may turn over the top card that is facing down. If you clear all the cards of a building stack, you may move any card or ordered sequence of one suit into that free space. Your goal is to build sequences of kings to aces in each individual suit, and once you build one, you may remove those thirteen cards from the playing area. If you can no longer move any cards, make sure there is at least one card in each of the ten building stacks and then deal ten cards from the stockpile, one on each stack. If there is an empty building stack, you must move a card or sequence of cards onto that area before dealing. The game ends when all eight sequences have been built and removed from the building stacks or when the stockpile is depleted and no further cards may be moved.

Variations of Spider

There are several variations to the game of Spider. In the variation called Scorpion, you use only one deck of cards and start with seven stacks of seven cards each. The first three piles contain three face-down cards and four face-up cards. The other four piles contain all face-up cards. The last three cards in the deck are the reserve. Play is the same, but only kings may be moved to a free space. When you can no longer play, deal the three reserves on the first three stacks, and continue play.

In the variation called Double Scorpion, you use two decks and play the game with the same rules as Scorpion. In Beetle, the initial stacks are all face up and visible. In Black Widow, any sequence of cards may be moved as a group, regardless of whether they are in the same suit.

The Game of Yukon

Yukon is extremely similar to Klondike. The difference is that a group of cards may be moved from stack to stack regardless of whether those cards are in sequence. Like Klondike, the objective of Yukon is to fill up the suit stacks, each stack with one suit from ace to king, using a standard deck of fifty-two cards. There are two areas of the playing field. The initial setup is the same as standard solitaire. The area across the top of the playing field is where you deal out seven building stacks. The first stack on the left has one card facing up. The second stack has one card face down, and the top card is face up. The third stack has two cards face down and the top card is face up, and so on, until the seventh stack, which has six cards face down and the top card is face up. The remaining twenty-four cards are then placed face up (four on each stack except for the stack farthest to the left). Also leave an area for the suit stacks, which will be four stacks of cards in sequence from ace to king, two built on either side of the Yukon setup.

Within the building stacks, a card may only be moved onto another card if it is of the opposite color and if the card it is being placed on is of the next higher value. The game differs from Klondike in that you can move multiple cards onto another card as long as the top card follows this rule. The cards do not have to be in a sequence to be moved. This makes the game easier to complete than Klondike because you are able to move many more cards around the playing field. A king has the highest value and may not be placed on any other number. If you clear the top card (facing up) from a stack, you may turn over the next card facing down to make it the new top card. If you clear all the cards of a building stack, you may move any card or ordered sequence into that free space. An ace may be moved to an empty suit stack and added to by placing the next value of the same suit on that card, building it up to a king. If you can no longer move any cards, you may turn over the first card in your pile of face-down cards and try to put it into play. If it cannot be played, or if you run out of plays within the playing field, you turn over the next card. The game ends when all fifty-two cards are in the suit stacks or when no further cards may be moved.

Chapter 4

Card Games for Two Players

Two-player card games are a great way to pass a quiet evening with a friend or family member. Cribbage is a popular, fast-paced card game that requires strategic discards and play. Bezique and piquet are older card games that both use shortened decks and variations of trick-taking skills. Tablanette is a quick game involving addition and the ability to foresee future plays. Spite and Malice is considered the two-player version of solitaire.

Cribbage

Sir John Suckling, an English poet and playwright, is credited with creating cribbage in approximately 1631. It's a fast-paced card game that uses a unique scoreboard called the cribbage board. The objective of cribbage is to be the first player to score 121 points or more, moving around the cribbage board twice and then crossing over the starting line with one or more points. The standard cribbage board has four parallel rows of thirty holes each, and there are two pegs for each player. You and your opponent use two rows each, moving up the outside row and down the inside row—completing a sixty-hole track. The two pegs are used to mark your current score (the one in front) and the previous score (the one in back). Each time you earn points, whether during play or in counting your hand, you move the rear peg ahead of the forward peg by as many holes as points earned. Each move is called a "peg," and you can peg one or more points per move.

Cribbage can be played with two players or with four players forming two teams with two players each. It uses a standard pack of fifty-two cards, with kings considered high and aces low. Cribbage opens with both players cutting the deck to see who will deal first. The player with the lowest card becomes the first dealer and deals six cards, face down, one at a time to each player.

Rules for Two-Player Cribbage

The game begins with you and your opponent looking at the six cards in your hands and each discarding two cards. The four discarded cards become the "crib" and are an extra hand for the dealer to use later. The dealer's opponent cuts the deck and turns the top card face up. This is known as the "starter" card. If it is a jack, the dealer scores and pegs two points. The starter card will be used again later to help you score points with your hand.

Play begins with the dealer's opponent laying down one card face up on the table. The dealer lays down a second card, adding the value of the two cards together to keep a running total. Each time a card is laid down, the cumulative value of your cards and your opponent's cards are added together into this running total. You can lay down any card that you wish, as long as the running total does not exceed thirty-one. You each keep your own cards in front of you instead of mixing the cards together. Play alternates between the two players. If you play a card that makes the running total exactly thirty-one, you peg two points. Your opponent then lays a card, and the running total starts over from zero. If you cannot play a card without exceeding thirty-one, you let your opponent know this by saying, "Go." If your opponent cannot play a card either, he pegs one point for the "go." If your opponent can play any cards without exceeding thirty-one, he plays those cards scoring one point for the "go" and an extra point if the new running total is exactly thirty-one. It is then your turn to lead a new card, starting the running total over at zero. This continues until you both have played your four cards. The last player to lay down a card pegs one point. The eight cards have been played, and now it's time to score the hand.

Scoring the Hand

Along with scoring the above points during play, you can score other points for different things, as follows:

- **Fifteens:** If you hit a value of fifteen in the running total, you score two points.
- **Pairs:** If you play a card of the same value as the previous card, you score two points.
- **Pair royal (three of a kind):** If you play a card of the same value as the previous two cards in a pair, you score six points.
- **Double pair royal (four of a kind):** If you play a card of the same value as the previous three cards in a three of a kind, you score twelve points.
- **Runs:** If you make a sequence of three cards (for instance, eight/nine/ten) you receive three points. If the run is four cards, you receive four points, and so on. The run does not need to be in exact sequence—that is, you could play a nine/ten/eight, which would still count for three points. The run can be made up of cards from any suit.

Cards played before the total resets to zero (after hitting thirty-one) do not count toward a pair, three of a kind, four of a kind, or run.

QUESTION?

What cards should I keep or discard?
The best cards to keep are fives, because they form fifteens with tens, jacks, queens, and kings, which are worth extra points. If it's your crib (deal), try to discard a pair or a sequence in the hopes of getting a run. If it's your opponent's crib, discard opposite cards and no fives or tens.

In proper cribbage etiquette, you each announce the running total and any points earned before pegging your score. For example, let's say you have a hand with 4♣ 5♠ 10♥ 7♥, and your opponent has a hand with 5♦ 6♣ 8♥ and 3♠. You lay down your 4♣ and say "Four." Your opponent lays down his 6♣ and says "Ten" because now the running total is four plus six. You lay down your 5♠ to make the running total fifteen, which scores you two points for fifteen and say "Fifteen for two." You peg two points on the cribbage board. Your opponent now lays down his 5♦, making the running total twenty and scoring two points for creating a pair. He says "Twenty for two" and pegs his two points. You lay down your 10♥, making the running total thirty and say "Thirty." Since your opponent cannot lay a card that will push the running total over thirty-one points, and he does not have an ace, he cannot play. He says, "Go." You score one point by saying "One for the go," and since you cannot play a card either, the running total starts again at zero and play returns to your opponent. He lays down his 3♠ and says "Three." You lay down your last card, the 7♥, and say "Ten." Your opponent lays down his 8♥, to make the final total eighteen points, says "Eighteen for one" because he laid the final card, and pegs one point.

ALERT!

When playing your cards, try not to lead with a five. This gives your opponent a good chance of adding a ten and scoring two points. It's also good to keep low-scoring cards in your hand in the hopes that your opponent will say, "Go," and you will be able to play.

Breaking Down the Points

After play is over, you each add up the points contained within the combination of your four cards plus the starter card originally turned up by the dealer. Each scoring combination (pairs, three of a kind, four of a kind, and run) scores the points stated. A flush receives four points if the starter card is not of the same suit and five points if it is. A nob (having a hand with a jack of the same suit as the up card) receives one point. You can also receive points that your opponent forgot to claim by calling "muggins" and declaring those points.

For example, suppose your hand has the cards 5♥ 5♠ 9♠ 10♥ and the starting up card is the J♦. You can form four combinations of fifteen (5♥ 10♥, 5♥ J♦, 5♠ 10♥, 5♠ J♦) and a run of three (9♠ 10♥ J♦) for a total of eleven points.

If you have a pair in a run, the run can be counted twice. Let's say your hand has the cards 2♦ 4♦ 5♥ 6♠ and the starting up card is 6♦. You have one run of 4♦ 5♥ 6♠ and one run of 4♦ 5♥ 6♦. You also have two combinations of fifteen 4♦ 5♥ 6♠ and 4♦ 5♥ 6♦, for a total of ten points.

The dealer's opponent adds up his points first, pegging them on the board, and then the dealer adds up his points and pegs. The dealer then takes the four crib cards, turns them over, and receives points for that hand as well. Any points he earns through those cards are scored and pegged immediately, before the next hand is dealt and played.

FACT

It is impossible to score nineteen points in a hand. So if you hear a player call out nineteen points, it refers to a worthless hand containing zero points. The player will then move his back peg to the hole right behind his front peg.

Order of Play

Order of play can become essential toward the end of the game, as each of you gets closer to winning. If you have enough points, you could go out before the dealer, even if the dealer has many points in his hand

and in the crib. If you beat your opponent before he reaches the last leg of the board, you "skunk" him and score twice as many points. If you beat your opponent before he makes his first trip around the board, you "double-skunk" him and can receive triple or quadruple points, depending on which variation you choose to play.

Cribbage with Four Players

If four people are playing, the players form two teams, with partners sitting across from each other. The dealer deals five cards to each player, who each discard one card into the crib. Play is the same as earlier, except if you say "Go," the three remaining players can play if able. The player who said "Go" is the first to lead the next card after all players have played. Teams score points as above, and team members peg their points sharing the same pegs. When scoring a hand, the dealer's opponents count first, followed by the dealer and his partner.

Bezique

Bezique originated in France and is thought to be a stepping stone to pinochle. Bezique moved to the United Kingdom and became very popular in the mid-nineteenth century. Custom cards were created for the game around 1862, and bezique markers and scorecards were introduced. Bezique is played with two players who try to score points during play by obtaining and declaring specific cards and groups of cards (as described later). It is played with two shortened decks of thirty-two cards, including the ace, king, queen, jack, ten, nine, eight, and seven of each suit. The rank of the cards from high to low is ace, ten, king, queen, jack, nine, eight, seven.

Rules of Play

A random dealer is selected and deals eight cards, face down, to each player in groups of three, two, and three. The remaining forty-eight cards are placed face down on the table to form the stockpile. The top card is turned over, and the suit of that card becomes the trump suit. If the card is a seven, the dealer scores ten points.

The dealer's opponent starts the game by leading the first card, laying down any card in his hand. The dealer then plays any card from his cards, and he is not required to follow suit or play a card from the trump suit. If he does not follow suit or play a trump, he automatically loses that round. If he plays a trump or a higher card in the suit that was led, he wins that round (called a "trick") and places those two cards face-down beside him. Whoever wins takes the top card on the stockpile, his opponent takes the second card, and the next card is turned over and placed on top of the stockpile for the winner of the next trick.

If a player wins a trick containing the seven of trumps, he may exchange it for the trump card that was originally turned over, in which case he receives a score of ten points. This is called a "declaration," and it can only take place after winning a trick.

During this stage of the game, you are not obligated to try to win the trick if you do not want the card on top of the stockpile and feel that the second (hidden) card might be of more help to your hand. After winning any trick, you may make a declaration (as described below). The winner of the trick leads the next trick by playing another card from his hand. You continue playing the cards and winning or losing tricks, always keeping eight cards in your hand, until the stockpile is depleted.

After the stockpile is depleted, you and your opponent each have eight cards in your hand and the final eight tricks are played. In these tricks, you must try to win the trick by playing a higher card in the suit led or playing a trump. If you cannot win the trick, you must still follow suit if able, or lastly play any other card from your hand. The player to win the final trick scores ten points. At the end of the hand, you also each score ten points for each brisque (ace and ten) collected in your tricks.

Declarations

You can score points during play for declaring specific cards and groups of cards. You may only make a declaration after winning a trick, by laying cards from your hand face down on the table. Cards that have been won and placed beside you cannot be used to make declarations. The available declarations are as follows:

- **Seven of trumps:** ten points
- **Common marriage (king and queen of same suit):** twenty points
- **Royal marriage (king and queen of trump suit):** forty points
- **Bezique (Q♠ and J♦):** forty points
- **Four jacks (one of each suit):** forty points
- **Four queens (one of each suit):** sixty points
- **Four kings (one of each suit):** eighty points
- **Four aces (one of each suit):** 100 points
- **Sequence (ace, ten, king, queen, jack of same suit):** 100 points
- **Royal sequence (A 10 K Q J of trump suit):** 250 points
- **Double bezique:** 500 points (two Q♠ and two J♦)

If the group of cards that you play is able to score two sets of points, you must declare one set of points after winning one trick, and then, on winning another trick, declare the second set of points. As an example, if you lay down the K♠ Q♠ J♦, you may take forty points for the bezique at that point and then twenty points for the common marriage on a further trick. Declarations, once laid down, are still considered to be part of the eight cards in your hand. You can play those cards on a future trick, and the player that wins that trick adds the cards to his pile of cards won. They are available for play on tricks or to make further groups of cards.

ALERT!

It is a standard rule that you may not make a declaration during the final eight tricks. All declarations must be made prior to the last card in the stockpile being taken, so make sure to declare any points early in the game.

Scoring is documented using either a cribbage board, paper, or special bezique markers that are made of wood and contain areas for marking scores. The first player to reach 2,000 points wins the game.

Piquet

Piquet is more than 500 years old and originated in France, where it was an extremely popular game for many years. The modern rules, established in 1882, are the same as those described here. Because it is a French game, many of the rules use French words and terminology. In piquet, the goal is to score more points than your opponent and to score 100 points or higher (called "getting over the Rubicon"). The game uses a shortened deck of thirty-two cards with the ace, king, queen, jack, ten, nine, eight, and seven of each suit. Aces are high, and sevens are low. You'll each cut the deck, and then whoever picks the highest card acts as the first dealer.

Deal and Discard

Dealing alternates between the players with each hand. Begin by dealing twelve cards, face down, in groups of two or three (dealer's choice). The remaining eight cards form the stockpile, or "talon," and are placed face down in the middle of the table. The dealer is known as the younger hand, and his opponent is known as the elder hand. If you are dealt a hand containing no court cards in any of the suits (jack, queen, or king), you may announce "carte blanche" and score ten points. You do this by rapidly dealing your cards face up on the table before you discard, as below. A new hand is then dealt.

> If the elder hand exchanges fewer than five cards with the talon, he may view the cards that he did not exchange in the talon. For instance, if he only took three cards from the talon, he may view the other two before his opponent takes them.

The elder hand discards anywhere from one to five cards face down and then picks up that number of cards from the talon. The younger hand then does the same, discarding anywhere from one to the number of cards not taken by the elder hand (if the elder hand discarded and took five cards from the talon, there are only three remaining for the younger hand). The players keep their discards next to them and may refer to them during play if needed for reference.

Scoring the Hand

The scoring of your hand is made up of three categories: the count of the hand, the count during play, and the extraordinary scores. Only the player with the best combination in each category scores for that category.

The hand is counted as follows:

• **Point:** the most cards in one suit. The number of cards in the suit is announced and the score is equal to that value.

• **Sequence:** the longest run of consecutive cards in one suit (requires a minimum of three cards). A sequence of three cards (tierce) scores three points. A sequence of four cards (quart) scores four points. A sequence of five cards (quint) scores fifteen points. A sequence of six cards (sixième) scores sixteen points. A sequence of seven cards (septième) scores seventeen points. A sequence of eight cards (huitième) scores eighteen points.

• **Set:** a group of cards of the same rank. Three aces, kings, queens, jacks, or tens (trio) scores three points. Four aces, kings, queens, jacks, or tens (quatorze) scores fourteen points.

FACT

You are not required to declare the highest sequence or set of cards that you hold. You can declare that you have a trio when in fact you hold a quatorze. This can help to throw off your opponent and is known as "sinking."

The elder hand begins by announcing his best combination in each category. You do not state the exact cards or suits—instead, you just give a number and/or the French term as above. After his announcement, the younger hand says "good" to signify that the elder's hand is better than his own best combination, "not good" to signify that he has a better combination, or "equal" to signify that the information is equal. If you say "equal," the elder hand must give more information about the suits or cards so that you can finally declare "good" or "not good." If the player with the winning sequence or set has multiple sequences or sets, he scores for each of those. If requested, you must show your winning combination to your opponent.

Playing Your Hand

After the elder hand has counted all of the points in his hand, he leads any card in his hand. The younger hand counts the points in his hand and then plays a card, following the suit of the elder hand if possible. The player who plays the highest card in whatever suit was led wins the trick and scores one point. Based on the declarations, you now have some idea of the cards in your opponent's hand, and he has an idea of what is in yours. You continue playing tricks, with the winner of the previous trick leading to the next one. Your goal during this stage of the game is to win as many tricks as possible in order to score points. Each time you win a trick, you score a point, and each time you lead a trick you score another point. After all the cards in your and your opponent's hand have been played, the player who won the most tricks scores ten points. If you each score six tricks apiece, neither of you scores the ten points.

There are also four sets of extraordinary points that can be won during play, as follows:

- **Carte blanche:** As discussed earlier, this is a hand with no court cards and scores ten points.
- **Pique:** If you score thirty points in hand and while playing your tricks, before your opponent scores any points—you win a "pique" and score thirty points. Only the elder hand can win a pique, as he scores one point for the first lead.
- **Repique:** If you score thirty points in hand alone, before playing any tricks and before your opponent scores any points, you win a "repique" and score sixty points. Either player can win a repique.
- **Capot:** If you win all twelve tricks, you score forty points (instead of the ten points for winning the most).

After the first hand has been played, you play five additional hands for a total of six, or a "partie." At the end of the partie, the player with the highest points subtracts his opponent's points from his own and adds 100 points. If one player does not score 100 points, he is "rubiconed." In this case, the player with the higher points adds both sets of points together and 100 points on top of that. The game is now over, and you can use your cumulative scores in tournaments or for future play.

Spite and Malice

Spite and Malice is a well-established card game that is often referred to as an interactive solitaire game for two people. Each player plays his hand one at a time, using cards that he and his opponent have previously played. The objective of Spite and Malice is to be the first player to get rid of the cards in your pay-off pile by placing cards in the center stacks in an increasing order. You'll be using two standard decks of fifty-two cards with aces as low, queens as high, and kings as wild.

FACT

Spite and Malice is often called a game of "Cat and Mouse," or the "Husband and Wife" game, because of the tit-for-tat play that you'll be following as you each complete your turns.

Rules of Play

A random dealer is selected and deals each player twenty cards, face down. Stack those cards into a pile, without looking at them—this becomes your "pay-off pile" that you want to get rid of to win the game. You are then each dealt five cards to your hand, and you can look at those cards. The remaining cards are placed face down to form a stockpile. There is an area to the side of you to hold four "hold" stacks that you will be discarding to later in play. In the middle of the table, between you and your opponent, there is an area for three center stacks.

Play begins with each of you turning over the top card in your pay-off pile. If the cards are of equal value, you'll each shuffle your pile and then turn over the top card again. The player with the highest value card plays first.

The player who goes first follows a couple of steps. If you have an ace, you'll want to play it to an open center stack. If you are able to lay down an ace, you can also build on that ace by placing a two, followed by a three, and so on, regardless of suit. The cards can come from your hand or from the top of your pay-off pile. Since your goal is to get rid of your pay-off pile, you will usually want to play a card from there first. Kings are wild and can be placed on any center stack, representing the next card in sequence. If you cannot play an ace, or when you can no longer add cards to the center stacks, your turn is over and you signify this by placing a card in one of your hold stacks. It is then your opponent's turn.

In future turns, you'll first check the number of cards in your hand. If you have fewer than five cards, you must draw cards from the stockpile to bring it up to five. You can then play cards on top of your opponent's cards in the center stacks, if he was able to play. You can use cards from your hand, from the top of your pay-off pile, or from the hold stacks. When your turn is over, you'll again discard a card to the hold stacks. There can only be four hold stacks at one time, so if all four have a card on them, the discard must go on top of a card, making the card underneath unavailable. You may play as many cards to the center stacks as you can, but as soon as you discard to a hold stack, your turn is over, and it's your opponent's turn to play again.

ESSENTIAL

If you are able to play all five cards in your hand, you immediately draw five more cards from the stockpile without waiting until your next turn. Your turn continues until you cannot play anymore and you place a card in the hold stacks.

If a center stack is complete (ace through queen), you shuffle it back into the stockpile, making room for a new stack to be built. Play ends when a player's pay-off pile has been completely moved to the center stacks. That player wins the game.

Variations of Spite and Malice

There are many variations to the game of Spite and Malice. You can play with more than two players by dealing out a different number of cards to the pay-off pile or by using additional decks of cards. You can also choose to play with more than the standard four center stacks, as many as you wish. Players can also choose to include the jokers and use them as wild cards. One variation during play is to require that the discard be placed on an empty stack, on a card with a similar value, or on a card that has a value one greater than the discard.

Tablanette

Tablanette is a unique four-deal game that involves addition, foresight, and strategy to discard the correct sequence of cards. Tablanette is played with two players, and the object is to discard your cards to pick up table cards and score points. The kings, queens, jacks, and tens score you points, along with the 2♣. The game uses a standard pack of fifty-two cards.

Rules of Play

The first dealer, who is randomly selected, deals six cards face down to each player and four cards face up to the middle of the table. If a jack is played face up, it is removed to the bottom of the stack and another card is dealt to the middle of the table.

The dealer's opponent starts by playing the first card. If a player lays down a card with a value equal to any of the four cards on the table, he picks up that card, leaving the card he played on the table. If any two or three cards on the table add up to the value of the card that was played, he can pick up all of those cards. During play, kings have a value of fourteen, queens have a value of thirteen, jacks have a value of zero, the number cards count as their face value, and aces can have a value of eleven or one. For example, you can lay down a king and pick up an ace and a three (counting the ace with a value of eleven). Or you can lay down a seven and pick up a six and an ace (counting the ace as a value of one).

The player then takes any card(s) he has removed and places it face down in front of him to create a pile. If he's able to take all of the cards on the table, he announces "Tablanette" and takes all those cards, including the card he laid down. This play is worth double points when it comes time to score the hand. The jack is a special card, and if you are dealt a jack, you can play it to pick up all the cards on the table. Since a jack is worth zero, you do not score any additional points on a Tablanette.

Players take alternate turns until all of their hands of six cards have been played. The dealer deals six new cards and play continues as above, followed by two more deals of six cards and play in between. If any cards remain on the table, the last player to take a card from the table gets to take the remaining cards.

Scoring the Game

Each player scores points for various cards that are captured during play. You score one point for the 2♣ and two points for the 10♦. You also score one point each for any king, queen, jack, or ten in your hand. If you have won more than twenty-seven cards, you score an additional three points. The first player to reach 251 points wins!

Chapter 5

Partnership Card Games

In a partnership game, four people play in teams of two. Typically, partners on each team sit across from one another around a four-sided table. The team scores are made up of a combination of the two players' scores. The majority of partnership games are played with the objective of forming melds or capturing tricks. Most partner games can be adapted to fewer or more players playing individually.

Canasta

Canasta (meaning "basket" in Spanish) was invented during the early twentieth century in Uruguay. The game was further developed in Argentina before arriving in the United States, where it became a huge fad during the 1950s. The objective of canasta is to score points by forming "melds," or groups of cards, consisting of three or more cards of the same value.

Canasta is played with four players making up two teams of two players; the members of each team sit across from one another. Two standard packs of fifty-two cards are used, along with four jokers. The jokers are each worth fifty points; aces and twos are worth twenty points each; kings, queens, jacks, tens, nines, and eights are worth ten points each; and sevens, sixes, fives, and fours are worth five points each. The jokers and twos are wild cards, and the threes serve special functions (as explained later).

FACT

Canasta is believed to have its roots in the game of 500 Rummy. With similarities in melding and in the ability to pick up the entire discard pile, it's easy to see how Canasta developed as a variation on that game.

Rules of Play

The first dealer is selected at random. When it's your turn to deal, shuffle the cards and have the player to your right cut them. Deal each player eleven cards, one at a time, face down. Place the remaining cards face down to form a stockpile. Turn over the top card of the stockpile and place it face up beside the stockpile to form the discard pile. If this card is a wild card or a red three, turn over the next card, continuing until the card is not wild or a red three.

Melds

Your goal while playing canasta is to collect cards to help you form and lay down melds. A meld in canasta consists of at least three cards of the same value. It must contain at least two natural (nonwild) cards, and no meld can contain more than three wild cards. A meld containing seven or more cards is called a "canasta" and scores you extra points. You must have at least one canasta to win the game, but you should try to build as many as you can. You cannot have a meld of the same value as your partner, so if you hold any cards that are the same value as one of your partner's meld, you'll just add your cards to his. In order to lay down your first meld(s), you must have a minimum number of points based on your team's cumulative score from the previous hands. If your team has a negative score, you need 15 points in your initial meld(s). If your score is 0–1,495, your team needs 50 points in your initial meld(s). If your score is 1,500–2,995, you need 90 points in your initial meld(s). If your score is 3,000 or higher, you need 120 points in your initial meld(s).

How to Play

Play begins with the player to the dealer's left and continues clockwise. When it's your turn, you start off by picking up either the top card in the stockpile or all of the cards in the discard pile (if it is not frozen, as described later). If you want to pick up the discard pile, you must first show that you can meld the top card with cards currently in your hand or be able to add the top card to one of your partner's melds. Remember that you can only make an initial meld if the cards you are laying down contain enough points based on your team's cumulative score. In the first hand, you have a score of zero and need fifty points in your initial meld. After laying down a meld, you can make additional melds if you wish. If you took the top card from the stockpile, you may also lay down any melds in your hand. You end your turn by discarding a card from your hand onto the discard pile.

ALERT!

Be careful not to get rid of too many cards in your hand early on in the game. This limits your options in being able to pick up the discard pile and obtain points. You'll want to lay down enough points in your melds to get the game going, but strategically hold a few back.

If your team has not yet melded any cards onto the table, or if the top card is a wild card or a black three, the discard pile is frozen and you may not take cards from it. The exception to this rule is if you have two natural cards in your hand and can use the wild card to create a meld.

If you draw a red three from the stockpile, you must place it face up on the table and draw a replacement card from the stockpile. Red threes score you additional points at the end of the hand, but they do not count as points toward laying down an initial meld. If you discard a black three, it freezes the pile until the next discard. The most important strategy in canasta is to be the first team to take the discard pile. This often lets you control the rest of the hand, pick up the pile often, and recycle black threes as discards.

Going Out

The end of the hand occurs with the first player to "go out." Your team must have at least one canasta before you or your partner can go out. To go out, you must meld all of the cards in your hand, or meld all but one card and use that card as a discard. If you hold any black threes in your hand, you may lay them down in a meld when you go out (the only time you may make a meld containing black threes). The meld must be three or four black threes and cannot contain any wild cards.

At any time that you are able to go out, you may ask your partner first by saying, "May I go out?" after taking a card from the stock or discard pile. Whatever your partner responds (yes or no) is binding, and you must abide by it. Your partner will most often answer with a yes to this question, but if he has extra points in his hand or is close to a canasta, he may ask you not to go out.

If your partnership does not have a canasta, you must manipulate your hand so that you have at least one card remaining after the discard. If you get rid of all the cards in your hand, you would go out illegally and would lose the game or score penalty points depending on what variation you choose to play.

Play immediately ends if the last card drawn in the stockpile is a red three, because there are no replacement cards for you to draw. If the final card drawn is not a red three, play can continue until a player does not wish to draw by taking the discard pile. The game would then end.

Scoring Canasta

Each team now scores their hand. You earn points for any cards you and your partner have melded, lose points for any cards in your hands, and receive bonus points as follows:

- Going out receives 100 bonus points.
- Going out "concealed" (without having laid any previous melds) receives an extra 100 bonus points.
- Each natural canasta (containing no wild cards) receives 500 bonus points.
- Each mixed canasta (containing wild cards) receives 300 bonus points.
- Each red three receives 100 bonus points if the partnership has at least one meld.
- Each red three is penalized 100 points if the partnership did not meld.
- All four red threes receive an extra 400 bonus points if the partnership had a meld, or –400 points if the partnership did not meld.

The winner of the game is the partnership that scores 5,000 or more cumulative points in a set, after several hands.

Variations of Canasta

There are many variations of canasta. You can allow play of a meld of entirely wild cards—a wild canasta would receive 2,000 bonus points. You can play with a limit on the number of cards taken from the discard pile. You can choose the option where a player cannot take the discard pile and just add the top card to a completed canasta—instead, he must use the top card along with cards in his hand. You can also rule that a player cannot take the discard pile to make a meld with one natural card and one wild card.

In two-player canasta, fifteen cards are dealt to each player. When a player draws from the stockpile, he draws the top two cards. In order to go out, a player needs two canastas. In three-player canasta, thirteen cards are dealt to each player. When a player draws from the stockpile, he draws the top two cards. The first player to pick from the discard pile plays the hand alone, and the other two form a partnership. At the end of the hand, the lone player gets his own points and the partners share their combined points, outside of red threes, which each player gets on his own.

Pinochle

Pinochle is a mid–nineteenth-century American game with similarities to the older European game of bezique. The objective of pinochle is to be the first team to score 500 points or more through bidding and playing multiple hands. Pinochle is played with four players forming two teams of two players, with the partners sitting across from one another. A deck of eighty cards is used containing four copies of each ace, king, queen, jack, and ten in the four standard suits. The cards rank from high to low as ace, ten, king, queen, and jack. A random dealer is chosen and deals out the entire deck, face down, one at a time, to all four players.

Bidding

A round of bidding begins with the player on the dealer's left. When it's your turn, you can choose to bid or pass. If you bid, you state the number of points that you plan to win in that hand. The opening bid must at least fifty points and every bid must go at least one point higher. If the bidding reaches sixty points, each bid must go at least five higher. If you pass, you are not allowed to re-enter the bidding. The bidding ends when three players pass. If the first three players pass, the dealer must bid. The highest bidder gets to choose the trump suit and it must be a suit in which the player has a marriage (a king and queen in that suit). If the high bidder has no suit with a marriage, the bidder's side loses points equal to the value of their bid and a new hand is dealt.

A bidding system can be established to convey information to your partner about the melds you have in your hand. A common system is that a jump in points while bidding represents ten melds. So if a player opens with a bid of 53, the "3" indicates to his partner that he has thirty melds.

Melding

After the trump is named, you and the other players each reveal any of your melds face up on the table. Possible melds and their values are as follows.

Pinochle Meld Values				
Meld	Single	Double	Triple	Quadruple
Run (A K Q J 10 of trump)	15	150	225	500
Royal marriage (K Q of trump)	4	8	12	16
Common marriage (K Q of nontrump)	2	4	6	8
Pinochle (J♦ Q♠)	4	30	60	90
Aces around (A of all 4 suits)	10	100	150	200
Kings around (K of all 4 suits)	8	80	120	160
Queens around (Q of all 4 suits)	6	60	90	120
Jacks around (J of all 4 suits)	4	40	60	80

Cards may be part of multiple melds at the same time, with the exception that a king and queen of trump may not be part of both a royal marriage and a run.

Playing Your Hand

The game begins with the highest bidder leading the first trick, laying down any one card from his hand or melds. Starting with the player to his left and continuing clockwise, you will each play one card to the trick from either your hand or the melds that you laid down earlier. The goal during this stage of play is to take tricks with aces, tens, and kings. When it's your turn, you must follow the suit of the card led and beat the highest card in play, if able. If you cannot follow suit, you must play a trump if able, and if a trump has already been played, you must beat that trump if you can. If a suit other than trump is led, and one of the other players lays a trump card, the remaining players may play a card of the original suit led and do not need to beat it. The player who lays the highest card of the suit led, or the highest trump, wins that trick and leads the next one. If two of the exact same cards are played, the first player to play the card outranks the second.

Scoring Pinochle and Variations

After all twenty tricks have been played, each team receives one point for each ace, ten, and king taken. The team who won the last trick receives another two points. Points from the melds are then added. If the side that won the bid scores at least as many points as it bid, both sides add their scores to their cumulative point totals. If the bidding side fails to make its bid, they receive negative points equal to the amount they bid and score nothing for their melds. The opponents keep their score for the hand and add it to their running total.

FACT

Because they score points, the ace, ten, and king are called "counters." The queen and jack are called "noncounters" since they do not contribute toward scoring points during the game.

There are several variations of pinochle, especially in the scoring of the game. You can pretty much choose to score the game however you would like—including counting kings and queens as five points, or counting aces, tens, and kings as 100 points instead of ten. Another variation is that after the bidding reaches 100, bid increments must be in tens. You can play that the bidding round only goes around the table one time. You can also play a variation in which the two players on the high bidder's team can exchange three cards simultaneously, face down, with each other.

Push

Push is related to the game of rummy, but it is played differently when it comes to drawing and discarding cards. Wild cards are also used to increase the potential meld options. The objective of Push is to get rid of as many cards in your hand as you can by creating melds of sets and sequences. Push is played with four players forming two teams of two, and with partners sitting across from each other. You play with two standard decks of fifty-two cards and four jokers. Jokers and twos are the wild cards.

Rules of Play

A game of Push has a total of five deals. The first dealer is randomly chosen. In the first deal, six cards are dealt one at a time face down to each player. The second deal gives seven cards to each player, the third deal gives eight cards, the fourth gives nine cards, and the fifth deal gives ten cards. The remaining cards are placed in a stack to form the stockpile. The top card of the stockpile is turned over and used to form the discard pile. If the card is a joker or a two, bury the card by placing it back in the stockpile and turn over another card. Deal rotates clockwise with each hand.

ESSENTIAL

If you notice that the player on your right is getting low in cards in his hand, it might be in your best interest to push some cards his way. The only downfall to this strategy is if you push him cards that he needs to go out!

The player to the dealer's left plays first and must complete a turn by drawing a card, melding if possible, and discarding a card. In order to draw a card, you can pick up the top card in the discard pile if you feel it adds value to your hand. Otherwise, you take the top card from the stockpile, put it on the top card of the discard pile and push it to the player on your left for that player to add to his hand. You then pick up the next card in the stockpile as your own and add it to your hand. After drawing a card, it is time to form any melds and play them on the table. A meld consists of a set of three or four cards with the same value or a run of three or more cards in a sequence in the same suit. A wild card may be used to replace a card in a set or sequence. You may meld your cards, add to other melds on the table, or replace a wild card with its natural card and use the wild card to form another meld on the table within that same turn. When your turn is complete, you must discard a card to the discard pile.

The first melds that you lay down must follow specific requirements, according to which hand is being played. For the first deal, the first melds you lay must be two sets of three cards. For the second deal, you must have one set of three cards and one set of four cards to lay as your first melds. For the third deal, you must have two runs of four cards in a sequence to lay as your first melds. For the fourth deal, you must have three sets of three cards to lay as your first melds. For the fifth deal, you must have two runs of five cards in sequence to lay as your first melds. Each hand is over when the first player gets rid of all his cards, either by melding the remaining cards in his hand or by melding all but one card and discarding that card at the end of his turn.

Scoring Push

When the first player goes out, the remaining players must add up the points in their hands by counting wild cards (twos and jokers) as twenty points each, aces as fifteen points each, tens and face cards as ten points each, and the three through nine as five points each. The score is added to any previous score, and the team with the fewest points at the end of the five hands wins!

Spades

Spades is an American card game that became popular on college campuses in the 1940s. Many sources state that spades originated from the game of whist, while incorporating play from bridge, euchre, pinochle and other trick-taking games. Spades is less complicated than its predecessors and has an easy bidding system, allowing fast-paced games and quick hands. The object of spades is to be the first team to make it to 500 points by making correct bids and winning tricks. Spades is usually played with four players forming two partnerships, with partners sitting across from one another. It can be played with two, three, or six players as well. You'll use a standard pack of fifty-two cards, counting aces as high and twos as low. Spades are always the trump suit, but the other suits are equal in value.

Rules of Play

A dealer is chosen at random, and she deals out the entire deck, face down, one a time, to all four players. In turn, each player must make a bid by stating the amount of tricks they hope (or expect) to take in that hand. The dealer's opponents bid first. You may discuss your bid with your partner, but you may not disclose any specific information about the cards or suits that you hold. You are not competing to get the highest bid, just stating a number of tricks. The player's individual bids are added together to form a team bid.

QUESTION?

May I tell my partner what cards I have?
No. When playing spades, you may not inform your partner of your exact cards. You can say that you believe you can take five tricks, but you cannot say, for example, that you have five high hearts in your hand.

Bidding "nil," or zero, means that you will not win any tricks during that hand. Any player may bid nil. The nil's partner will bid the number of tricks he will take. If your team is 100 points behind, you can bid a "blind nil," which must be declared before you look at your cards. Then, after you've looked at your cards, you're allowed to exchange two cards with your partner by choosing two cards from your hand and passing them face down. Your partner looks at those cards, and returns two cards from his hand face down.

The game begins with the dealer leading the first trick by laying down any one card in his hand. Play continues clockwise around the table.

THE EVERYTHING CARD GAMES BOOK

When it's your turn, you must follow suit if you can or discard any one card of another suit from your hand. The player who played the highest card in the suit led, or the highest spade, collects that trick and leads the next one. You may not lead spades unless a spade has been "broken" (played on a previous trick) or you have no other suit in your hand.

Scoring Spades

After all the cards have been played, the teams score their hands. If you captured the number of tricks (or more) that you bid, you receive ten points for each trick bid and one point for each extra trick won. (For example, if you and your partner bid seven tricks between you, and together you won eight tricks, you win seventy points for the tricks you bid plus one point for the extra, or seventy-one points.) If you did not capture the amount of tricks bid, you lose ten points for each trick that you bid. If you bid nil and won no tricks, your team receives a bonus of 100 points. If you bid nil but won one or more tricks, your team loses 100 points. A blind nil receives a bonus or penalty of 200 points, depending on if you won any tricks or not. The first team to score 500 points over multiple hands wins the game.

ALERT!

If your team accumulates ten or more overtricks over the course of several hands, you are considered to be "sandbagging" and lose 100 points. (In other words, once the last digit of your score reaches nine, you will lose 100 points the next time you take an extra trick over what you bid.) After that, if you accumulate ten more overtricks, you lose another 100 points, and so on.

Variations

There are several variations of spades. You can play that each team must bid a minimum of two tricks or four tricks, or that you may increase your bid after seeing what the other team bids. You may choose an option where the combined bids of both teams may not total thirteen, forcing at least one of the partnerships to not win their exact bid, or that each partnership must have one nil bidder.

62

When playing spades with three players, the 2♣ is removed from the deck of cards. You deal each player seventeen cards, and then everyone declares a bid of how many tricks they think they can individually win. Rules of play and scoring are the same. When playing spades with five players, you remove the 2♣ and 2♦ from the deck of cards. You deal each player ten cards, and then everyone declares a bid of how many tricks they think they can individually win. Rules of play and scoring are the same. When playing spades with six players, you form three teams of two players each, with partners sitting opposite one another. You use two decks of cards, minus both 2♣. Rules of play and scoring are the same, except if there is a tie in cards laid down, the second player to lay down the card beats the first.

Rook

Rook is popular mostly in Canada and the United States, especially in eastern Kentucky, Pennsylvania, Ohio, southern Ontario, and Manitoba. The objective of Rook is to be the first team to score over 500 points by winning points taken through tricks.

Rook is played with four players divided into two teams, with partners sitting across from each other. A special Rook deck of fifty-seven cards is typically used. The Rook deck consists of cards numbering one to fourteen in four colors (red, green, yellow, and black), plus a Rook card. If you do not have a Rook deck, you can use a standard deck of fifty-two cards plus a joker. (The game description below assumes that you do not have a Rook deck, but if you do—just add an extra trick during play and score the one as fifteen points.)

Rules of Play

A dealer is selected and deals out thirteen cards to each player. He then places the final card in the center of the table. Deal passes to the left with each hand. A round of bidding begins with the player to the dealer's left. When it's your turn, you may pass or bid a number that reflects the amount of points you believe your team can earn through collecting tricks.

The bid must be a multiple of five, and the minimum bid is seventy. There are 200 points available in each hand. Aces are worth 15 points, kings are worth 10 points, tens are worth 10 points, fives are worth 5 points, the joker is worth 20 points, and the winner of the last trick wins 20 points. Bidding continues around the table until three players pass. If a player passes, she cannot bid at any further point in the bidding round.

> **ESSENTIAL**
>
> You should probably not bid if you have zero aces in your hand. There is one exception to this. If you have a long suit (six or more cards of the same suit), you can consider bidding and call that suit as trump.

Play begins with the high bidder taking the card in the middle of the table and placing it face down in front of him, without looking at it. His team collects any points that the card is worth after the hand is over. You now each choose three cards from your hand to pass to your opponent. Simultaneously you all pass your cards to the player on your left (in the next hand, pass to the player on your right and then back again). Without looking at the cards passed, the high bidder calls the trump suit and may then look at the cards that were passed to him.

The high bidder decides if he would like to lay the first trick or have the player to his left begin. Whoever goes first may lay down any one card in his hand. Play continues clockwise around the table. When it's your turn, you must follow suit, if you can, by playing a card of the same suit that was led. If you cannot follow suit, you may play any card. The trick is won by whoever played the highest card of the suit led, or the highest trump played. The Rook, or joker, is the lowest trump card. The winner of each trick leads to the next one.

Scoring Rook and Variations

After all the cards have been played, each team calculates their points as above. If the high bidder's team wins the value of the points bid, they score their bid. If they win all of the tricks, they receive a bonus of 100 points. The opponents receive the amount of points for the cards they won as well. If the high bidder's team does not earn enough points through their tricks to equal the value of points bid, they lose points equal to the amount of their bid. The opponents keep the points they won. The first team to reach 1,000 points wins the game.

There are several variations of Rook. You can play with five people, where the high bidder calls out a "partner card" of his choice and the player with that card becomes the high bidder's partner. The partner does not reveal himself until he plays that card. At the end of the hand, the high bidder and his partner individually receive half of their combined points. The other three players receive their individual points.

Other variations include starting with a minimum bid of seventy-five instead of seventy, not passing three cards before playing the hands, or playing to 500 points instead of 1,000. In another version of Rook, there are no extra points for winning the last trick, so only 180 points are available per hand.

Chapter 6

E Games for Larger Groups

Card playing is a very social event. What better way to liven up a get-together than by breaking out a deck of cards? The games in this chapter are tailored to provide fun and competition for larger groups of people, typically involving four or more players. You'll find games that involve betting, bidding, and even a game that bases your social status on the order in which you and the other players won the hand.

The Game of Twos

Also known as Deuces, Big Two, Big Deuce, Choh Dai Di, or Dai Di, Twos is a relatively new game, created in China around 1980. It is a very strategic game, meaning you must think ahead in order to be successful. The objective of Twos is to be the first player to get rid of your cards (and to try to have as few cards in your hand when another player goes out). Twos is played with two to four players using a standard pack of fifty-two cards. The cards rank from high to low as two, ace, king, queen, jack, ten, nine, eight, seven, six, five, four, and three. The suits rank from high to low as spades, hearts, clubs, and diamonds.

Rules of Play

The first dealer is selected and shuffles the cards. The player to the right of the dealer cuts the deck and then exposes a card. Count counterclockwise to that value to determine which player is dealt the first card. For example, if the exposed card was a four, the dealer counts four players from him in a clockwise direction, and that's the first person he deals a card to. Then deal the entire deck out counterclockwise. There are four types of play in Twos, and a play can only be beaten by a better combination of the same number of cards. The first type of play is Single Cards. A higher-ranked card beats a lower card, and if the two cards are of equal value, the higher-ranking suit wins. The second type of play is Pairs, in which there are two equal-ranking cards. A higher pair beats a lower pair, and if two pairs have the same value, the higher-ranking suit wins (as an example, 4♠ 4♣ beats 4♦ 4♥). The third type of play is Three of a Kind, in which there are three cards of equal value. A higher three-of-a-kind beats a lower three-of-a-kind. The fourth and final type of play is Five Cards. These are five cards with descending rank as follows:

• **Straight flush**—Five cards in sequence within the same suit. The rank of the highest card determines the winner, and if they are of equal value, the rank of the suit determines the winner. Twos are counted normally in straights (rather than as high card).

- **Four of a kind**—Four cards of equal value. A higher four-of-a-kind beats a lower one.
- **Full house**—A three-of-a-kind and a pair. A higher three-of-a-kind determines the winner.
- **Flush**—Five cards in the same suit. A higher suit rank determines the winner, regardless of the highest-value card.
- **Straight**—Five cards in a sequence of mixed suits. The rank of the highest card determines the winner, and if they are of equal value, the rank of the suit of the highest-value card determines the winner.

The game begins with the player who holds the 3♦. You play this card either by itself or in a combination as above. Going around the table clockwise, each player in turn must pass or beat the previous play by laying down a higher value combination of the same number of cards. This continues until all players have passed. The pile of cards is turned over and the player who laid the last combination starts by laying a new play of any number of cards she chooses. Again, all players in turn must pass or beat that play by playing a higher-value combination of the same amount of cards. The first person to discard all of his cards wins, and the game is scored.

QUESTION?

Do I have to play if I'm able?
No, you're not obligated to play a hand if you are able. You can pass and then jump back in the game at a further point in the same round or in a different round if the opportunity arises.

You receive a penalty for the cards remaining in your hand after another player goes out. Cards with a value below ten receive one point each, and cards with a value ten or above score two points each. If you hold your original thirteen cards, you receive thirty-nine points in penalty. The majority of players play Twos for money, and at the end of the game, the losers pay the winner the difference between their points.

Variations

There are multiple variations of Twos that can be played. Deal can start to the dealer's left or right instead of cutting the deck, and you can play the game clockwise instead of counterclockwise. Four-of-a-kind can be played as a four-card hand instead of a five-card hand. You can play that if a player passes, he cannot play the rest of the round. If you have only one card remaining in your hand, you must announce it. One last option is to play so that if you have twelve cards in your hand at the end of the game, you receive thirty-six points.

The Game of 727

The game of 727 is one of competition, but you don't exactly know whom you're competing against. The objective is to obtain a hand with a value as close to seven or twenty-seven as possible. The winners of the hand are the two players closest to those two numbers. So if you're the only person going for the lower hand, you actually don't have any competition! A game of 727 requires four to ten players who use a standard pack of fifty-two cards. Kings, queens, and jacks are worth half a point each. Numerical cards are worth their face value. Aces can be worth one or eleven points.

Rules of Play

Players start by placing an ante into the pot. The dealer deals one card face up to each player and then deals one card face down to each player. You view your cards and then, when it's your turn, you may ask for an additional card, which is dealt face down.

Play begins with a round of betting, starting with the player to the dealer's left. You may either check (pass) or bet by adding money to the pot. If you pass, the next player has the same options. This continues around to the dealer. If everyone passes, the betting is over.

If any player bets, the remaining players may "fold" their hand and abandon play, "call" by adding the same amount of money to the pot, or "raise" and put the amount initially bet plus an additional amount of money into the pot. This continues around the table until everyone has folded or the stakes are equal for all remaining players. If all players fold, the player who initially bet wins the pot, and the next dealer deals.

> The game of 727 is a bizarre mixture of poker and blackjack attributes. There are multiple rounds of betting similar to playing a hand of poker, but the object is to get closest to a specific value, is in the game of blackjack.

After this round of betting, if you are still in the game, you can ask for an extra card. If any player requests a card, there is another round of betting and another round of asking for cards. This continues until no player asks for another card, and the game moves to a showdown.

In the showdown, all players who have not folded display their cards. The winners are the player who has a hand with a value closest to seven *and* the player who has a hand with a value closest to twenty-seven. These players split the money in the pot. If there is a tie for seven or twenty-seven, those players split their portion of the money.

Variations

There are multiple variations of 727. Each player can initially be dealt two cards face down and one card face up. You can also rule that if a player has points that total more than twenty-seven, he busts and his score doesn't count. Another option is that in the case of two hands equally close to the score but in different directions (one has six and one has eight, for example), the player with the lower total wins. You can also add jokers to the mix of cards. If a joker is dealt up, it makes your down card have a negative value. If a joker is dealt down, its value is equal to the number of cards you have.

Brag

Brag is a British card game that is similar to poker but with an unusual betting style and hand rankings. The objective of Brag is to win money from each hand by betting and playing your cards strategically. Brag requires three to eight players and uses a standard pack of fifty-two cards. All suits are equal in value. The hand rankings, each containing three cards, from best to worst, are as follows:

- **Prial**—three of a kind. The highest-ranking prial is all threes, followed by aces, then kings, down through twos.
- **Running flush**—a straight flush (a three-card sequence of cards within the same suit).
- **Run**—a straight. The highest-ranking running flush or run is 3 2 A, followed by the typical order of A K Q, K Q J, and so on.
- **Flush**—three cards within the same suit. In case of a tie, the flush with the highest-ranking card wins.
- **Pair**—two-of-a-kind and a single card. In comparing pairs, the higher-ranking pair wins.
- **High card**—three cards of different values.

FACT

The odds of receiving a prial of threes are 5,524 to one. The odds of receiving a prial of another value or a running flush are 459 to one. Remember these odds when building your hand.

Rules of Play

Players begin by placing their antes in the pot. A dealer is selected and deals three cards face down to each player. A round of betting then takes place. Play starts with the player to the dealer's left, who can either bet or fold his hand. If there was a previous bet, you must add at least that much money to the pot. Unlike poker betting, money that you added in previous bets to the pot is not taken into consideration. For instance, if you bet three chips and Player 2 then folded, then Player 3 bets three chips, and the remaining players (including you) must bet three chips to stay in the game.

Betting continues until there are only two remaining players. At this point the player who is next to bet may double the previous bet to "see" his opponent, and his opponent has to lay his hand down first. If your hand beats his hand, you show your cards to prove it. If your hand ties or is less than his hand, you throw in your cards and lose the pot. If you choose not to see your opponent, he may choose to see you. If neither person chooses to see the other, both hands are displayed at the same time and the better hand wins the pot.

Playing Blind

You may opt to play your hand blind, without looking at your cards. When you do this, your bets cost half as much as an open player's (a player who has viewed his cards). You may choose to look at your hand before any bet, but then your hand becomes open and you must bet equal amounts going forward. If you are one of the two last players and playing blind, the open player may not see you.

ESSENTIAL

Unless a hand is "seen" and won by a prial, the cards are not shuffled in between hands. Instead, the cards are added to the bottom of the stack of cards, and the dealer deals the new hand from the top.

If all of the players fold to you as a blind player, the pot remains, a new ante is played, you keep your previous hand, and you are dealt a second hand. At any time, you may choose to look at either hand. At that point, you decide whether to keep that hand or throw it away. If you keep the hand that you looked at, you throw away the other hand and are now open. If you throw the hand away that you looked at, you keep the other hand and are still blind. If everyone folds to a blind player who has not looked at either pair of cards, at the next deal he must throw one hand away without looking at the cards.

Variations

There are multiple variations of Brag. In Four-Card Brag, four cards are dealt to each player. You view your cards and discard one of the cards to make a Three-Card Brag hand. In Five-Card Brag, five cards are dealt to each player, and you discard two cards to make the best Three-Card Brag hand. You can also play with wild cards, options including making twos, black twos, one-eyed jacks, the suicide king (K♥), or jokers wild.

Fan Tan

Fan Tan is an easy game that uses a solitaire-like layout of cards. With more players, the pot can build up quickly because each player has fewer cards and less chance of play. The objective of Fan Tan is to get rid of all the cards in your hand. Fan Tan can be played with three to eight players, but is best with four to six players. A standard pack of fifty-two cards is used, with kings high and aces low.

You and your opponents cut the deck, and the player with the highest-value card deals first. After you each contribute two chips to the pot, the dealer deals the entire deck, one at a time, face down to each player. Deal then passes to the left for each hand.

Play begins with the player to the dealer's left laying down a seven in the middle of the table. If he does not have a seven, he must contribute one chip to the pot. The next player may then play a six or eight of the same suit as the seven played, or a seven of a different suit. The six is placed on top of the seven, the eight beneath the seven, or the seven to either side of the first seven. The next player can then play off any of the cards available, by placing cards of a higher or lower value on the same suit, or laying down another seven, and play continues clockwise. If at any time you cannot play to the table, you must contribute a chip to the pot. The resulting display is a grid of four columns in each suit, running from low to high. A sample matrix after twelve plays might be the following:

		5♣	5♥
6♦		6♣	6♥
7♦	7♠	7♣	7♥
8♦		8♣	
9♦			

If you are able play a card to the table but fail to do so, you may be caught during play later on in the game. Since you cheated and did not play as required, you would owe three chips to the pot.

If you have a high or low card in any suit, it makes the most sense to play a six, seven, or eight in that suit early on so that others can build, and you can then play your high or low cards. Otherwise, try to play cards that leave the fewest openings for your opponents. The first player to get rid of his cards wins the game and takes the pot.

Hearts

Hearts derives from Reverse, a Spanish game where the jack and queen of hearts scored players negative points if captured. You play individually, rather than in partnerships, and many people prefer this cut-throat style of action. The objective of hearts is for you to try to get the lowest score by avoiding taking tricks containing hearts and the queen of spades (which are worth points). This is the extreme opposite of trick-taking games because the goal is to lose tricks, not to win them. Hearts is usually played with four players using a standard pack of fifty-two cards. Aces are high, and twos are low.

Rules of Play

A random dealer is selected and deals out the entire deck, face down, one a time, to all four players. You each select three cards from your hand to pass to another player. On the first hand you simultaneously pass the three cards to the player on your left, on the second hand to the player on your right, on the third hand to the player across from you, and on the fourth hand you pass no cards. After that, the cycle is repeated.

The game begins with the player who has the 2♣ placing that card face up on the table. Play continues clockwise around the table. You each lay one card on the table, following suit if you are able, or playing any other card in your hand if you have none of that suit. On the first trick you may not discard a heart or the Q♠. The player with the highest card in the suit led collects that trick and leads the next one. You may not lead hearts on a trick unless a heart or the Q♠ has been played on a previous trick or you have no other suit in your hand.

When choosing which cards to pass to another player, pass the ace, king, and queen of spades if you have fewer than four spades, as otherwise you might be forced to take the queen if spades are led. You should also get rid of diamonds or clubs if you have fewer than four cards in either suit. You can then get rid of hearts early on if those suits are led.

Scoring

After all thirteen tricks have been played, you add up the number of hearts in the tricks you have collected—the number of tricks doesn't matter. Each heart is worth one point, and the queen of spades is worth thirteen points. If a player takes all of the hearts and the queen of spades, he "shoots the moon" and scores zero points while all other players score twenty-six points. The game ends with the first player to reach 100 points. The player with the lowest score at that time wins the game.

Oh Hell!

Oh Hell! is also known as Elevator, Blackout, Up-and-Down the River, and other various names. There are a fixed amount of hands played, rather than playing to a specific point value, and the objective of each player is to strategically bid the exact amount of tricks he plans on taking. Three to seven players are needed to play Oh Hell! using a standard pack of fifty-two cards. The cards in each suit rank ace, king, queen, jack, ten, nine, eight, seven, six, five, four, three, two. The trump suit beats any value of a nontrump suit.

Rules of Play

A dealer is determined by each player drawing cards. The player with the highest card becomes the first dealer, and the deal then rotates clockwise. The number of cards that you deal out is based on what hand of the game is being played. In the first hand, each player is dealt one card, in the second hand two cards, in the third hand three cards, and so on. This continues until you reach a hand where the number of cards dealt would not be distributed evenly (one or more players would have one fewer card than another). When you reach that hand, you start decreasing the number of cards dealt to each player by one. Deals continue in this decreasing order until the final hand is dealt with one card to each player. For example, for four players, there are a total of twenty-five deals. The first deal has one card, up through the thirteenth hand with thirteen cards dealt to each player. Then the hands decrease back to one. With five players, there are a total of nineteen deals, and the maximum number of cards each player receives is ten.

After the cards have been dealt, you turn the next card face up. The suit of that card is considered trump for that hand. In a hand where there are no leftover cards, the hand is played with no trump. The game begins with players bidding the number of tricks they believe they can win in that hand. You may bid zero if your objective is to take no tricks. The dealer is the last to bid and must never bid a number of tricks that would cause the cumulative number of tricks bid from all players to equal the number of tricks available. The hand must always be over or under bid.

FACT

The hook in the game of Oh Hell! is that at least one player must fail each hand because the total number of tricks bid is not equal to the number of tricks available. Thus the name of the game.

The player to the left of the dealer begins by playing one card from his hand. Each player in turn must follow that suit if he can. If you are unable to follow suit, you may play any card in your hand. The player who laid the highest card in the suit led, or the highest trump, wins that trick. That player then leads the next trick. Play continues until all cards have been played.

If you win exactly the number of tricks that you bid, you receive ten points for each trick. If you bid zero and did not take any tricks, you win ten points. If you miss your bid, you lose ten points for each trick that you were under or over your bid. At the end of all of the hands, the player with the highest cumulative score wins the game.

Variations of Oh Hell!

There are multiple variations of Oh Hell! The hands can be dealt with no trump suit. In dealing the hands, you can deal each hand with one more card until the maximum is hit and stay there for the remaining number of hands, or you can start in a decreasing order from the maximum down to one and back up to the maximum again. In choosing the trump suit, you can allow the player who bid the highest to determine the trump suit or to call no trumps. In scoring, you can subtract the number of points bid if the player wins fewer tricks than he bid, subtract the number of tricks taken if the player wins more tricks than he bid, or add ten points plus the number of tricks bid if the player wins exactly the number of tricks that he bid.

In the variation called Boerenbridge, the rules are slightly changed. The objective of the game is to hit 100 points exactly. If you go over 100 points, your score is deducted a value of points equal to the amount that you went over. (For instance, if your score was 104, you would deduct four from 100, causing your score to become 96.) The entire pack is dealt out for each hand, and everyone makes a bid at the same time. Each player get one point for each trick won and a 10-point bonus for getting the exact amount of tricks bid. If a player bids zero tricks and takes zero, she receives a 20-point bonus. When a player's score reaches eighty, he does not take part in the bidding and only receives one point per trick won.

President

If you've ever wanted to be president, or at least have control over your friends and family, this game is for you! The objective of President is to get rid of all your cards as fast as possible because the order of winners determines a player's social status in the next hand. Just make sure you're not the last player to go out, or you have to obey everyone else at the table. This game is also known as Bum, Scum, Butthead, Capitalism, and other derogatory names. Four to seven players are needed, along with a standard pack of fifty-two cards. The cards rank from high to low as two, ace, king, queen, jack, ten, nine, eight, seven, six, five, four, three. The suit is irrelevant.

Rules of Play

The first dealer is selected and deals the entire deck face down clockwise around the table. Some players may have one more card than other players. Future deals will be determined by the order of winners in that hand.

The game begins with the player to the dealer's left. He may play any single card or any group of cards of the same rank by placing the card(s) face up on the table. Play continues clockwise and each player may either pass or play a card or group of cards, dependingon and equal to the number that the first player led, that beats the most recent play. Any higher single card beats the previous single card, or a higher group containing the same number of cards beats the previous group of cards. It is not necessary to beat the previous play just because you can, and you can always pass.

Play continues until someone makes a play and everyone else passes. All the cards played are then turned face down and placed to the side. The player who played last starts a new round by playing any single card or any set of cards of the same value. If a player whose turn it is to play has no more cards in his hand, the turn passes to the next clockwise player.

Social Status

The first player who is out of cards is awarded the highest social rank for the next hand (President). Next is Vice President, Citizen, or whatever names you choose to designate around the table. The last player is the Scum, Peasant, or other term of choice. The players of higher status are entitled to use their power over the lower-ranking players.

For the next hand, the players move seats. The President selects the premium location, the Vice President sits to the President's left, all the way around to the Scum, who sits to the President's right. The Scum becomes responsible for all menial tasks, including shuffling the cards, dealing, and clearing them away as necessary. Since the players are now seated in order of their rank, and the Scum is dealing, the first card is dealt to the President. When the deal is complete, the Scum gives his highest card to the President, and the President returns a card he does not want. The President then starts the game.

Variations

There are many variations of President. Instead of leading the game with the player to the dealer's left, the player holding the 3♣ leads the first hand of the game. In playing the game, a card with equal value can beat the previous card, and you are not required to play an equal number of cards to the card or group initially dealt. This means that a pair beats a single card and three-of-a-kind beats a pair. You can add jokers, which are the high cards, or have the ace as high instead of the two. If you keep the two as the high card, then playing a single two can beat a pair, and a pair of twos can beat a three of a kind. While playing, if you are able to beat the previous play, you must do so instead of having the option to pass. A four-of-a-kind means an inverse of rank, so now in each turn you must play a lower card or set. After you pass, you are no longer able to play that round.

Chapter 7

Card Games for Kids

Kids love playing card games, especially when they are able to win against their friends and family! Give them a chance to foster their competition by teaching them, and then playing, one of these many card games. It's an excellent way for them to learn how to match numbers, add and subtract, and even gain teamwork skills. Who knows, they may beat you on the very first play with their skill and speed!

52 Pickup

If you're really looking for a way to really annoy your card partner, suggest a game of 52 Pickup. This is not actually a card game, so it's nice to know the rules if you've never played before. This is a game that helps to develop humor and organization skills. Two or more players are needed to play the game, and you'll use a standard pack of fifty-two cards. Multiple packs can be used for more cleaning fun! The player to suggest the game removes the cards from the deck and asks another player if he wants to play. If any other player accepts, the first player throws the cards up in the air so that they fall, completely scattered, on the floor. It is then the job of the other player(s) to pick up the cards and organize them. That's it, game over!

Crazy Eights

Looking for a strategy game to play with your little ones? Crazy Eights involves thinking ahead and planning for your last discard. It also develops matching skills, following suit, and recognizing the value of cards. The objective of Crazy Eights is to be the first person to discard all of the cards in your hand. Two or more players are needed to play this game, and you'll use a standard pack of fifty-two cards.

Rules of Play

A dealer is randomly selected and deals five cards face down to each player, if there are multiple players, or seven cards if there are only two players. The remaining cards are then placed face down in a stockpile, accessible to everyone in the playing area. The top card is turned face up and placed next to the stack of cards to start the discard pile.

The game begins with the player to the dealer's left. If the first card turned over in the discard pile is an eight, the player chooses a suit and then discards a card of that suit from his hand. If the card is not an eight, the player discards a card of that suit *or* of that value from her hand. For instance, if the top card is 6♦, you may discard a six of any suit or any diamond. If you have no cards that can be played, you must pick up the top card from the stockpile. The next player to the left then plays, with the same options. If you discard an eight, you must then call out a new suit for the next player to play. The game stops when any player discards the last card in her hand.

ALERT!

If you have an eight in your hand, you might want to save it until the last card. This strategy assures that you will be able to discard your last card without having to wait for a suit or value to match that card.

Variations

You can choose to score the game, in which case the remaining players with cards in their hands get penalty points when someone goes out. They receive fifty points for an eight, ten points for a face card, and face value for any numerical cards. You keep score until a player reaches an agreed-upon score (typically 100 or higher) and the player with the lowest score wins. There are a few more variations to Crazy Eights. More than five or seven cards can be dealt to each player. You can continue picking up cards from the stockpile until you are able to play a card. During play, if an ace is laid down, the direction of play is reversed until another ace is played.

Go Fish

Go Fish is a fun, classic game of trying to steal the best cards from your opponent's hand to complete pairs in your own. This game requires two to six players, playing with a standard pack of fifty-two cards. The objective of Go Fish is to reel in the most matching pairs of cards, while helping to develop pairing and matching skills.

Rules of Play

A random dealer is selected, who deals six cards face down to each player. The remaining cards are placed face down in the center of the table. Play begins with all players laying down any pair(s) of cards that they have in their hand. Then the dealer is first to act. He gets to ask another player for a card of a specific value in the hopes of making a pair with a card in his hand.

If the player has that card he must give it to the person who asked, and he places that card with the matching card in his hand and lays them down. He may then ask another player for a card. Anytime a player does not have the card that he's asked for, he says, "Go Fish," and the player who asked takes a card out of the pool on the table. If the card picked up is the card asked for (a catch), he places the pair down and may ask another player for a card. If it is not the card asked for, his turn ends and it is the next player's turn. Play continues in the same fashion around the table until one player's hand is gone or the pool is drained. The player with the most pairs wins the game.

Variations

There are several variations of Go Fish. In one variation, a player must collect all four cards (a "book") before laying them down. Therefore, in play, you will ask another player for "all of" the card that you wants (that is, "Give me all of your threes"). Instead of taking cards out of the pool, you can play with a stockpile, and if the player has to go fish, he takes the top card. In the variation called Authors, players must ask for a specific card including its suit—"Give me the queen of hearts" instead of "Give me your queens."

Memory

Also known as Concentration, Memory is a game of . . . well, just that! The game requires players to remember where previous cards are positioned in order to make a match. This game is played with two to four players and a standard deck of fifty-two cards. The objective of Memory is to collect the most matching pairs of cards.

A random dealer is selected, and he shuffles the cards and deals all of the cards face down in a grid pattern. The game begins with the first player turning over two cards, keeping them in their original position on the grid. If you make a match, you collect that pair and may turn over two more cards. If they do not match, you turn those cards back over, and it is the next player's turn. The player to the left repeats the process. Play continues until the grid is completely gone. The player with the most pairs wins the game.

If you turn over a card and you think you know where the match is, turn over your guess first. If you got mixed up and didn't remember correctly, you still hope to make a pair by turning up another card and seeing if it makes a match.

I Doubt It

If you're good at bluffing, I Doubt It is the game for you! The objective of I Doubt It is to be the first to get rid of your stack of cards. This game requires two or more players, using a standard deck of fifty-two cards, and helps to develop counting skills and the ability to recognize the value of cards.

A random dealer is selected who deals out the entire deck evenly to the players. Play begins with the youngest player laying face down on the table any number of aces in her hand. As she lays them down, she calls out what they are ("Two aces"). The next player then discards any or all of his twos, the next player his threes, and so on until kings are played. After you play kings, play continues on again to aces.

Since the game ends when the first player gets rid of his hand, a player will undoubtedly yell, "I doubt it" when you lay your last card. Make sure that it's a correct call, or you'll be stuck picking up the discards and possibly losing!

Since you are laying your cards face down, you can actually bluff your opponents. You can lay down a four but say that you are laying down a ten. If you believe that another player did not lay down the cards he said he did, yell out "I doubt it!" The player then has to turn over the cards he laid down. If they are indeed the cards he said they were, you must pick up the entire pile of discarded cards. If the cards are different than what he said, he must pick up the pile of discarded cards himself! The first player to get rid of her cards wins the game.

Old Maid

Nobody wants to be the Old Maid! That's the mission of this game, to get rid of all of your cards so that you're not the last player stuck with the Old Maid card. Old Maid requires two or more players and helps to develop matching and pairing skills. You'll want to use a special Old Maid deck of cards, or a standard pack of fifty-two cards minus one of the queens.

A random dealer is selected and deals out all of the cards out clockwise around the table. Players then discard any pairs that they have in their hand. The dealer then begins play by offering his cards face down to the player on his left. That player may choose any of the cards displayed and add it to her hand. If this card makes a pair with any other card in her hand, she discard that pair. She then offers her cards to the player on her left. You are safe and out of the game once you have discarded all of the cards in your hand. Play continues until only one player is left holding the Old Maid card (or the last queen). That player becomes the Old Maid and loses the game.

FACT

A traditional Old Maid card deck contains matching cards of various occupations. The Old Maid card is the elderly, single woman without a matching card. The remaining occupations are considered much more acceptable and won't make you the loser.

Slap Jack

Slap the jack, and don't make the mistake of slapping another card! If you're the first to slap a jack, you win all of the cards on the table. The more cards you collect, the closer you are to winning the game. The objective of Slap Jack is to collect the entire deck of cards, while developing awareness and fast response skills. This game requires two to six players, and you'll use a standard pack of fifty-two cards.

A random dealer is selected, and he deals out the entire deck evenly to all players, face down. You each make a neat stack with your cards and place the pile directly in front of you. The game begins with each of you simultaneously turning over a card from your deck. If a jack is played, the player to first slap the card wins and collects all cards on the table. The player then places those cards at the bottom of her stack. You all continue to turn over the cards simultaneously until another jack is played. If you run out of cards you can stay in the game by watching the others discard and being first to slap the jack. If you slap a card that is not a jack, you must give a card to each of the other players. The game ends when one player has all of the cards.

Speed

If you're fast at laying down your cards, and you can match them to the next higher or lower number, then Speed is the game for you! Make sure to slip your card in before your opponent's so that you can fulfill the objective and get rid of your cards to win the game. Speed helps to develop rapid responses, sequence recognition, and suit recognition skills. Only two players can play this game, using a standard pack of fifty-two cards.

Setting Up the Table

A random dealer is selected, and he sets up the playing area. In the center of the playing area, two cards are dealt face down next to each other. On the top and bottom of these cards, five cards are dealt, face down and next to each other. The remaining cards are dealt face down to each player. The game begins with both players turning their respective five cards over and yelling "Go!"

Getting Rid of Your Cards

You both immediately turn the two cards in the middle over. You may then place any of your five cards on the stacks of two cards, as long as your card has a value one above or one below the top card in that stack, regardless of suit. An ace can be played on a king and vice versa.

You can play on either stack of cards. Whenever you play one of the five cards in your hand, you may replace it from your stack of face down cards. When neither you nor your opponent can play on the two stacks, play stops. You each then take the top card from your face-down stacks and place that card on top of the stack of two cards. Play immediately begins again. The speediest player to get rid of all her cards wins!

FACT

In Speed, each player can only use one hand at a time, and he can move only one card at a time. If he uses both hands to move cards, he automatically loses because this gives him an advantage over his opponent.

Spoons

Spoons, also known by the name Pig, is a fun, silly game to play with both children and adults. The objective of Spoons is to grab a spoon before they are all gone, while developing value recognition skills, matching, and visual awareness. Three to thirteen players can play this game, using a standard pack of fifty-two cards and a bunch of spoons. Before playing the game, you'll want to place a group of spoons equal to the number of people playing minus one, in the middle of the circle of players.

I Want a Spoon

A dealer is randomly selected and deals four cards to each player. He then places the remainder of the cards on a pile to his left to create the stockpile. Play begins with each of you simultaneously passing one card to the player on your left. The dealer takes a card from the stockpile, and the player to his right places a card in a discard pile . . . but the remaining players are all passing cards, one by one, to the player on their left. You can pass as fast as you would like, but you can only have four cards in your hands at a time, and you may only pick up and pass one card at a time. If you're the first player to get a four of a kind, you can take a spoon from the center of the table. As soon as one player takes a spoon, the other players may each take one. The last player to attempt to take a spoon will be unable to do so because there aren't enough spoons to go around. That player is the loser for that round.

QUESTION?

May I be sneaky about taking a spoon?
Absolutely! If you are the first player to get four of a kind, try to sneak a spoon as if you were picking up a card or passing it. It's much more fun to see if anybody else notices before grabbing the spoons out of the center of the table. If you notice a player take a spoon first, try to be sneaky when you take yours as well.

Variations

There are multiple variations of Spoons. Players can play without a stockpile. If you play without a stockpile, you must play with a modified deck of four cards for each player. For example, if you are playing with five players, you'll want to have a deck of four aces, four kings, four queens, four jacks, and four tens. The dealer now takes a card from the player on his right, instead of playing with stock and discard piles.

Another option of play is to deal five cards to each player. In this game, the player has five cards in his hand and only needs to have four of a kind out of the five cards to pick up a spoon.

In the variation called Pig, no spoons are used. Instead, the first player to get four of a kind quietly places his finger to the end of his nose. When another player notices this, he should touch the end of his nose, whether or not he has four of a kind. The last player to touch his nose is the loser and becomes the pig. This game can be played with or without a stockpile.

Players can also play a series of games, with the loser of each game sitting out the next round. Just make sure to remove a spoon each game.

War

War is a classic card game enjoyed by both kids and adults. It is an easy game to learn and helps to develop matching and value recognition skills.

In War, you battle your opponent and hope that you beat her card as you try to collect the entire deck. Be careful, though, or you might just lose your highest-ranking cards and lose the game. War requires two players, and you'll need a standard pack of fifty-two cards.

A random dealer is selected, and he shuffles the cards. He then deals out the cards, one at a time, face down to each player. You both will have twenty-six cards that you keep face down in a neat pile in front of you. Play begins with both of you turning over your top card. Speed is not a factor in this game, so there's no need to flip over your card quickly. The player who has the highest-ranking card gets to keep both cards. He turns those cards over and puts them face down at the bottom of his stack. You both then turn up your next card. Again, the player who has the highest card gets to take both cards. An ace takes a king, and a queen takes a six, and so on. The stacks will continue to grow, shrink, and grow again.

ALERT!

In order to win the game, you have to get the aces. Since aces are the highest cards, a lower card cannot beat it in a battle one on one. If you don't have an ace, you'll have to win one in an all-out war.

When you both turn up cards with an equal value, it's time for a war to break the tie. You'll each lay three cards face down and a final card face up. Whoever has the highest tiebreaker card wins the hand and claims the spoils of war—all eight cards. If the tiebreaker cards are of equal value, you'll have another battle and continue to do so until there are two different cards, and one player wins all of those cards. The player who collects the entire deck wins the game.

War can also be played with three or four players. The entire deck is dealt out, and during play the high card takes the other cards. When two cards match in a value, war breaks out, and all players participate—not just the two players with matching cards.

Chapter 8

Whist

Whist originated in England and has been around for quite a long time. It is considered the stepping stone to learning and playing the game of bridge and is easily understood by beginning card players. There are many variations of whist played across the globe, so this chapter teaches you the history of whist, strategies for winning, and the rules of standard whist, Bid Whist, German Whist, Knock-Out Whist, and Minnesota Whist.

History of the Game

Whist has its roots in two card games from the early seventeenth century, Ruff and Honors (English) and Triomphe (French). First a game played by the lower classes, it was taken up by higher-class gentlemen in approximately 1718. Whist was an extremely popular card game through the nineteenth century, taking second place only to euchre and later to bridge. Experts say that Louis XV, Napoleon, Queen Victoria, Benjamin Franklin, Ulysses S. Grant, and Edgar Allen Poe were all known at one time or another to play whist! Whist is no longer a commonly played game in the United States, but it is still recognized in England and is played in local tournaments called "whist drives."

Standard Whist

Standard whist is played without a round of bidding on a trump suit. Instead, a card will be turned up, and the suit of that card will be considered trump for that hand. To play whist you'll need four players who are divided into two teams, with partners sitting opposite one another. You'll also need a standard pack of fifty-two cards—aces are high, twos are low. During play, the objective of whist is to take as many tricks as possible in each hand. Teams only receive points for each trick over six that they win.

Rules of Play

A random dealer is chosen, and if you are the dealer, have the player to your left shuffle the cards. Have the player to your right cut the cards. Now take the cards and deal them out one at a time, face down, to each player until you reach the final card in the deck. This card is turned face up and is used to determine the trump suit. The card remains on the table until your first turn, when you pick it up and add it to your hand.

The game starts with the player to the dealer's left laying his first card face up on the table, choosing any one card in his hand. Play continues clockwise around the table with each player laying a card of the same suit that was led. If you cannot follow suit, you may play any card, including a trump. The person who played the highest card of the suit led or the highest trump wins the trick. The winner of each trick leads the next trick.

At the end of the thirteen tricks, the team with more than six tricks receives one point for each trick over six. The first team to reach five points wins the game and the team to win the best two out of three games (a rubber) wins.

ALERT!

If you fail to follow suit when you have cards in your hand that are able to do so, this is called a "revoke." The penalty for this action is three points and can either be added to your opponent's score or deducted from your team's score, depending on how you choose to play the game.

Variations

There are multiple variations of whist that put a fun twist on play. In the game of Honors, a bonus is received if a team holds all four honors (ace, king, queen, and jack of the trump suit) at the end of the hand. If a team holds three of the four trumps, they receive two bonus points. In the American version of whist, the first team to win seven points wins the game. No rubber is played. In the variation of Long Whist, the first team to win ten points wins the game. In the game of Trumps, the trumps are fixed for each hand. The trump suit alternates through the four hands, and a no-trump hand can be played for the fifth hand if desired.

Bid Whist

Bid Whist is an African-American tradition that is thought to have originated in the United States during the period of slavery. Jokers were added as the highest trump cards, and the players determine the rank of the individual cards during a bidding process. The bidding round also determines whether there will be a trump suit, what that trump suit is, and the scoring of the game based on the number of tricks a team feels it can win. The objective of Bid Whist is to take as many tricks as possible in each hand through strategic play with your partner. In order to play Bid Whist you'll need four players divided into two teams, with partners sitting opposite one another. You'll also need a standard pack of fifty-two cards plus two jokers.

The two jokers that you use must be easily differentiated from each other. You'll assign one a title of "big joker" and the other the title of "little joker." The big joker becomes the highest trump, and the little joker becomes the second-highest trump during play.

A Round of Bidding

A random dealer is selected and deals the cards one at a time, face down, until each player has twelve cards. The remaining six cards are then placed face down on the table to form a "kitty," which is a group of cards that will come into play later in the game.

After the deal, there is one round of bidding. The player to the dealer's left either passes or makes a bid containing a number and the term "high," "low," or "no trump." In some games, "high" might also be called "uptown" or "straight," and "low" might be called "downtown" or "special." The number in the bid represents the number of tricks that you believe your team can take in excess of six tricks. High means that your team will declare the trump suit and that high cards win the tricks. Low means that your team will declare the trump suit and that low cards win the tricks. No trump means that there will not be a trump suit in that hand, and after bidding, your team will determine if high cards or low cards will win each trick.

Each consecutive player may choose to bid or pass. If you bid, your bid must be higher than the previous bid. You can bet a higher number than the previous number bid, or bid no trump to beat the same number low or high. While bidding, you do not name which trump suit you are going to call if you win the bid. If the first three players pass, the dealer must bid.

After bidding is complete, the high bidder names the trump suit, or, if the winning bid was no trump, the high bidder declares whether the game is going to played high or low. The high bidder then picks up the kitty and discards six cards in any combination from the cards in his hand and the cards in the kitty. These six cards are placed face down in front of the bidder and are considered the first trick won.

A low bid and a high bid have the exact same value. Therefore, a three high does not beat a three low. You must bid a higher number than the previous number bid, or you can bid no trump to beat a high or low bid.

Rules of Play

The high bidder starts the play by laying down his first card face up on the table. He may play any card in his hand. Play continues clockwise around the table. When it's your turn, you must follow suit, if you can, by laying down a card of the same suit that was led. If you cannot follow suit, you may play any card, including trump.

The trick is won based on the type of bid won. If a trump was declared, the cards rank depending on whether the bid was high or low. The trump suit always beats another suit, and within an individual suit the rank is big joker, little joker, ace, king, queen, jack, ten, nine, eight, seven, six, five, four, three, and two for a high game. For a low game, the rank is big joker, little joker, ace, two, three, four, five, six, seven, eight, nine, ten, jack, queen, and king. If a trump was not declared, the cards rank as above without the trump suit beating any of the other suits, and jokers have no value. The winner of each trick leads the next one.

If the winning bid was no trump, and you lead a trick with either of the jokers, the next player to your left determines that trick's suit with the suit of the card that he plays. Each player must then follow that suit if he can.

Scoring Bid Whist

After the hand is played, each team counts their tricks. If you are the bidding team and win the number of tricks you bid (the number you bid plus six), you receive a point for each trick won above six. If you did not win the number of tricks you bid, you must subtract a value equal to the number of tricks bid from your score. If your team bid a no trump, the points gained or lost are doubled. The opposing team receives zero points for that hand, regardless of what happens with your team. The first team to score seven points wins the game.

A bid of seven high, low, or no trump is called a Boston. Since the number that was bid is added to six, this means that you are attempting to win all thirteen tricks. One variation of the Bid Whist scores quadruple points on a Boston if the bid is won.

ALERT!

If a team reaches a score of negative seven points, they automatically lose. This method of losing the game, versus losing when their opponents reach seven points, is called "going out the back door."

Variations

There are many variations to Bid Whist. A player can start with a bid of four, instead of three. If the winning bid is no trump, players must discard their jokers and pick up a new card from the kitty (after the winning bidder has picked up the cards and discarded their six cards). Another variation is if the winning bid is no trump, a player may play a joker at any time, even if they have a card within the same suit as the suit led. If the game is played with only one joker, the kitty only has five cards. If the game is played with no jokers, the kitty only has four cards. In one variation, the 2♠ is also a trump card and is below the little joker in value. A scoring variation is that the opposing team scores points if the bidding team fails to make their bid, instead of the bidding team receiving negative points.

Contract Whist

Contract Whist is different from other versions of Whist in that it includes a bidding round in which players bid the number of tricks they believe they can win. In each successive hand, the number of cards dealt is decreased by one. You'll need at least three to six players to play the game of Contract Whist. You'll also need a standard pack of fifty-two cards. Aces are high, and twos are low. Your objective is to take as many tricks as you bid by strategically playing your cards and paying close attention to your partner.

A random dealer is selected and deals the maximum amount of cards so that each player has an equal value (thirteen cards for four players, ten cards for five players, and so on). Deal passes to the left, and the number of cards dealt in each successive hand decreases by one on each deal. The final hand will be played with only one card dealt to each player.

After the deal, there is one round of bidding. The player to the dealer's left starts by bidding the number of tricks he believes he will be able to take with his cards. Each player in turn also bids the number of tricks she believes she can win. You do not need to beat the previous bid. The dealer also bids, but may not bid an amount that will allow the total of all bids to exactly equal the amount of tricks available.

Trumps are predetermined in Contract Whist, cycling through hands in the following order: spades, hearts, diamonds, clubs, and no trumps. The player to the dealer's left leads the first trick by laying down any one in his hand. Play continues clockwise around the table. When it's your turn, you must follow suit if you can. Otherwise, you play any other card in your hand. The highest card in the suit led, or the highest trump, wins the trick. The winner of each trick leads to the next.

There are two variations of scoring. In one variation, you receive one point for each trick won and ten bonus points if you score your exact bid. In the other variation, you only receive points (one point for each trick won, plus ten bonus points) if you score your exact bid. If you do not score the exact bid, you receive zero points regardless of how many tricks you won. The player with the most points after ten deals wins the game.

German Whist

This variation of whist is played with only two players using a standard pack of fifty-two cards. Aces are high, and twos are low. The game is split into two stages of play. The objective of the first stage is to set up your hand for the second stage. The object of the second stage is to take as many tricks as possible.

Rules of Play

A random dealer is selected, and that player deals thirteen cards face down to both players. The remaining twenty-six cards make up the stockpile and are placed face down on the table. The top stock card is turned up, and this becomes the trump suit. The two stages are then played out.

In stage one, if you're the dealer, your opponent lays down his first card. He may play any card in his hand. You must follow suit if you can, by playing a card of the same suit that was led. If you cannot follow suit, you may play any card. The trick is won by who-ever played the highest card of the suit led, unless a trump was played, in which case the highest trump wins. The winner of the trick takes the top card from the stockpile and the other player takes the second card. The next card in the stockpile is turned face up and another trick is played. The winner of that trick takes the top card from the stockpile and the other player takes the second card. The tricks won in this stage do not count toward winning the game. Play continues until the stockpile is gone.

The strategy of the first stage of German Whist is to try to win the trick if you want the visible top card on the stockpile, or lose the trick if you believe the second card has a better chance of helping your hand.

In stage two, you'll proceed to play out the remaining thirteen cards in your hand and try to win each trick. If you have a good memory and are able to count cards, you should now know exactly what cards are in your opponent's hand. This allows you to play strategically and win multiple tricks. After all the cards have been played, the player with the most tricks won during stage two wins that game.

Variations

One variation of German Whist is that the tricks won in the first stage also receive points and count toward winning the game. This involves a different strategy, as you won't want to necessarily give up a trick in the hopes that the next card of the stockpile is better for your hand. Another variation involves the initial deal. Each player receives eleven cards in their hand and a "box," which is four cards face down. A player cannot look at his box until he wins a trick. After that, he can play out of the box if he is unable to follow suit from his hand.

Knock-Out Whist

Knock-Out Whist is an exciting game in which the number of cards in each successive hand decreases by one, as in Contract Whist. The objective of Knock-Out Whist is to be the last person standing to win the game, or the person to win the last trick on the last hand. You'll need two to seven players and a standard deck of fifty-two cards. Aces are high, and twos are low.

Rules of Play

A random dealer is selected and deals out seven cards, face down, to each player. He then turns over the next card, and the suit of that card becomes the trump suit. There will be seven deals in total, and with each deal the number of cards will decrease by one. The second deal is six cards to each player, the third deal is five cards to each player, and so on until one player has won or until the deal has reached one card. The next game is dealt with seven cards again.

The player to the dealer's left starts by leading the first trick. Play continues clockwise around the table. When it's your turn you must follow suit, if able, or play any other one card from your hand. The player with the highest card in the suit led, or the highest trump, wins that trick and leads the next one. All seven cards are played, and the hand is over.

After the first hand, the second dealer deals out six cards, face down, to each player who is still in the game. The player who won the most tricks during the previous hand gets to call trump for this hand, after looking at his cards. The hand is played as above, and the next hand is dealt with one fewer card.

If you did not win any tricks in a hand, you are awarded the "dog's life," meaning that you are dealt only one card on the next hand while the remaining players are dealt the standard number of cards for that hand. You can choose to play that single card on whichever trick you want and if you win that trick, you are back in the game. If you lose that trick, you are out of the game. If two players are knocked out during the same round, they both get a "dog's life." Each player to be knocked out after any one or two players receive the "dog's life" is out of the game for good. The winner is the last player standing or the player to win the trick of the last hand (when only one card is dealt to each player).

ALERT!

If two players make it to the last deal, with only one card each, it's the luck of the draw who will win. The player to win more tricks in the previous hand will call trump as the suit of the card that she holds. If her opponent has a card higher in that suit, he wins. If he has a card in another suit, or a lower card in the suit called, he loses.

Minnesota Whist

Minnesota Whist includes a bidding system in which the players choose whether they want to play offense, by attempting to win the game with seven or more tricks, or defense, by winning the game with six or fewer tricks. The objective of Minnesota Whist is to take as many tricks as possible in each hand if the game is played high or to take as few tricks as possible if the game is played low. To play this game you'll need four players divided into two teams, with partners sitting opposite one another. A standard pack of fifty-two cards is used, with aces high and twos low. No trump is played in this game, so suits are of equal value.

A Round of Bidding

A random dealer is selected and deals the cards one at a time, face down, to each player until all cards are dealt. Each player should now have thirteen cards.

A round of bidding begins to determine how the game will be played. If a hand is played high, the team must take seven or more tricks. If the hand is played low, the team must take six or fewer tricks. If you want to play high (or grand), signal this by laying down a low black card from your hand. If you want to play low, lay down a low red card from your hand. The player to the dealer's left turns over his low card first. If it is red, the next player turns over his card. As soon as a player turns over a black card, all bidding stops and the hand is played high. If all bidding cards are red, the hand is played low. The first team to display a black card is "granded."

Rules of Play and Scoring with a High Bid

The player to the right of the person who granded the bids starts the game by laying his first card. He may play any card in his hand. Play continues clockwise around the table. When it's your turn you must follow suit, if you can, by playing a card of the same suit that was led. If you cannot follow suit, you may play any card.

FACT

In order to save time, some players use two decks of cards. While the dealer is dealing out one hand, his partner shuffles the other deck and places it to his right so that the next dealer is ready to deal the next hand.

The trick is won by whoever played the highest card of the suit led. He then leads the next trick. The score is determined by giving the team that won more tricks, one point for each trick won over six tricks. The first team to reach thirteen points after multiple hands wins the game.

Rules of Play and Scoring with a Low Bid

The player to the left of the dealer starts the game by laying his first trick. He may play any card in his hand. Play continues clockwise around the table. When it's your turn you must follow suit, if you can, by playing a card of the same suit that was led. If you cannot follow suit, you may play any card. The trick is won by whoever played the highest card of the suit led. He then leads the next trick. The score is determined by subtracting one point for each trick won over six tricks. The first team to reach thirteen points over multiple hands wins the game.

Winning Strategies

Whist is a team game, so in order to win you must communicate with your partner and be supportive of her choices. Partner games can be tricky, so pay attention to what your partner is playing and follow accordingly. If you win the bid, throw out your first card from the suit you are strongest in. This will be a signal to your partner. If you are not the player to win the bid, a way to signal to your partner that you are strong in one suit is to throw out your lowest card in that suit when you are unable to follow another suit. This shows your partner where you will be able to help. You must also pay attention to the first card thrown out by your partner so you know where his strength lies! Unfortunately, if you have no strengths and play a card, your partner might assume that you're indicating strength when you aren't.

If your partner is leading a trick, you'll want to follow his lead. If he plays a high card, you'll want to play your lowest card—it doesn't make sense to waste his high card by playing one over it. If he plays a low card, you'll want to play a high card to win the trick.

If you win a trick, you'll want to play all of your winning cards before handing the lead back to your partner. You'll also want to try to pick up all of the trumps before playing an alternate suit. This allows you to determine what remaining trump cards there are in the game.

If you are playing a no-trump hand in Bid Whist, pay close attention to the cards your partner is playing! If you are not going to try to win the trick, play your lowest card in the suit led. There's no sense in throwing away cards that might be useful to you later. An exception to this rule is that if you only have two cards left in a suit, throw the high one first and the low one second. This is a signal to your partner that you are out of that suit and can now play trump.

Chapter 9
Bridge

Bridge is a complex game with a strategy that revolves around when to bid or pass, counting cards, and communicating with your partner. It's also one of the most popular card games around. This chapter explains the history of bridge, the four phases of each hand in bridge (dealing, bidding, playing, and scoring), and the standard strategy behind bidding each hand. You'll also learn a couple of variations of bridge to shake things up a little.

History of Bridge

Bridge developed from the card game whist. The name of bridge is said to come from Russian Whist, called "biritch." In the 1890s, bridge was brought over and introduced to U.S. card aficionados. In the 1900s, a trump suit was added, and a spin-off of auction bridge was introduced. In this method of bridge, a team received points toward winning the game for every trick won above their contract. Across the years, many additional changes were made to the game, but in 1925 Harold Vanderbilt codified the game of contract bridge along with its rules, procedures, and a scoring table. Since the 1930s, contract bridge has been one of the most popular card games played in the world. The difference between contract and auction bridge is that in contract bridge, any tricks above the contract are bonus points rather than helping toward winning a game. The majority of players adopted Vanderbilt's methods, and today there are millions of contract bridge players. Most people play at home, but there are over 1,000 tournaments a year and 4,200 bridge clubs that players can join! The rules for contract bridge are presented in this chapter.

Dealing a Hand

Bridge is a team, or partner, game made up of four players divided into two teams of two players sitting across from one another at the table. The players at each table are described by the compass directions: North, East, South, and West.

ESSENTIAL

It is proper etiquette to wait until the dealer deals out all the cards before picking up your hand. This gives everyone the same amount of time to view their hand, sort their cards, and determine their strategy for bidding.

Bridge opens with any player shuffling the cards and spreading them on the table face down. You each select a card in the middle (not taking any of the four outer cards), and the player who draws the highest card becomes the first dealer. Deal then rotates clockwise around the table for each successive hand. The dealer begins with the player on his left and deals the cards clockwise, one at a time, face down, to each player until he reaches the final card in the deck.

Bidding

After the deal you'll participate in a round of bidding to determine who will be the "declarer," or the player with the highest bid who gets to declare the trump suit. The player to the dealer's left starts the bidding by either passing or making a bid containing a number and the suit he wishes to have as trump. The number in the bid represents the number of tricks that you believe you can win in excess of six tricks—for example, you bid two, and this means you will win at least eight (six plus two) tricks. When bidding, the suits are ranked from high to low as no trump, spades, hearts, diamonds, and clubs.

Player Choices

When it's your turn, you may choose to bid, pass, double, or redouble. If you bid, your bid must be higher than the previous bid. You can do this by betting a higher number than the previous number bid, or by bidding the same number with a higher suit than the previous suit bid. The lowest bid is a one club, and the highest bid is a seven no trump.

If all four players pass on their first turn around the table, the hand is "passed out." The cards are thrown on the table, and it's the next dealer's turn to deal.

Within the bidding process, you may double a bid by the opponent's team or redouble the opponent's double. This increases the score or penalty for that bid. If you double or redouble, and another player bids a number or suit higher than the previous bid, your double or redouble is canceled out.

After a player bids and the other three players pass, the bidding stops. The last bid becomes the contract that the bidding team must try to make. The player who made the high bid becomes the declarer, and his goal is to complete the contract. The declarer's partner is the "dummy."

Am I out of the game if I pass?
No. If you pass, you are not out of the game. If bidding continues around the table to you again, you can pass again, or now you can bid, double your opponent's bid, or redouble your opponent's double.

Bidding Example

The bidding can get relatively complicated, so you'll want to make sure you understand the rules before participating in a game. The best way to learn is to watch a couple of rounds of bridge before playing yourself. The following is an illustration of bidding, with North as the dealer.

North	East	South	West
	1 ♥	2 ♣	Pass
Pass	2 ♥	Double	Pass
Pass	Pass		

East becomes the declarer, and West becomes the dummy for this hand. The contract is two hearts, meaning that the trump suit is hearts and the declarer must win eight tricks (the number bid plus six) in order to complete the contract. The contract is also doubled, which has implications on the way the hand is scored, as described below.

Rules of Play

After the round of bidding has finished and the contract has been decided, it's time to play out your hands. Your object during this round of play is to capture as many tricks with your partner as you can. If your team contains the declarer and has the contract, you need to win your contract or risk losing many points. If your team did not win the contract, your goal is to prevent your opponents from winning so that you can gain their points. The player to the left of the declarer starts the play by laying down his first card. He may play any card in his hand.

ALERT!

To make bridge a five- or six-player game, remember that only four people can play at a time. The fifth and sixth players will sit out until a rubber has been won, and then they will rotate in based on the order that they drew cards for the original deal.

Dummy's Hand

Immediately following the opening card, the dummy must expose his cards by laying them face up on the table, facing the declarer. You should place each suit in its own column with the cards in that column sorted by rank and overlapping each other. The trump suit should be on the left-hand side when the declarer views the cards.

If the trump suit of this hand was hearts, a sample dummy hand as viewed from the declarer would look like:

10 ♥	K ♠	J ♦	8 ♣
7 ♥	10 ♠	6 ♦	7 ♣
4 ♥	5 ♠	3 ♦	
	3 ♠	2 ♦	

Following Suit and Winning the Trick

Play then proceeds around the table, and each player needs to lay down a card, following suit if he can. If you cannot follow suit, you may play any card, including a trump suit. If you are the dummy in any hand, when it's your turn to play, the declarer states which card to play and you will play it (or the declarer may just place the card himself). If the declarer only calls out a suit for you to play, you must play the lowest card in that suit. As the dummy, you are not allowed to speak or otherwise communicate with the dealer during the remainder of the hand.

The trick is won by whoever played the highest card of the suit led unless a trump was played, in which case the highest trump wins. If the dummy wins the trick, the declarer tells him which card to lead for the next trick (or plays it himself).

ALERT!

If you are the declarer, be careful when touching the dummy's hand. If you touch any card, it is considered played, except for the initial arranging of the cards. As you take tricks, you want to organize them in front of you so that the number of tricks won is clearly visible to all players.

The following is an example in which the trump suit is hearts, North is the declarer, and East leads the first card. On the first trick, the players play the following cards:

North	East	South	West
A♦	2♦	4♦	8♦

In this first trick, each player was able to follow suit and did so. Since the highest card within the suit was the A♦, North wins the trick and leads the next card, and the other players follow.

North	East	South	West
4♣	2♣	A♣	5♣

As with the first trick, each player was able to follow suit and did so. The highest card was the A♣ that the declarer played out of the dummy's hand, so the declarer won a second trick. He must now lead out of the dummy's hand.

North	East	South	West
K♦	3♥	3♦	6♦

In this third trick, East wins the trick because he played a trump card and beat the other cards in the hand. If the hand had been bid no trump, then East would not have been able to win the hand with a card from any of the suits other than diamond.

Scoring

You win Bridge by winning two out of three games (known as a rubber). The first team to score 100 points wins each game. Once you have won a game, you are considered vulnerable and are subject to higher bonuses and penalties in the second game than your opponents, who are not vulnerable.

The scorekeeper keeps score on a piece of paper divided into two columns and two rows (imagine a plus sign drawn through the paper). The columns are separated into each team marked "we" and "they." The rows are separated into the scores won for contracts and the scores obtained for bonuses and/or penalties. The contract points go on the bottom half of the page (below the line), and the bonus/penalty points go on the top half of the page (above the line).

Scoring the Contract

If the declarer completes the contract, he receives a score for each trick in excess of six tricks. The tricks receive points based on the trump suit that was declared. If the trump suit is clubs or diamonds, each trick bid receives twenty points. If the trump suit is hearts or spades, each trick bid receives thirty points. If there are no trumps, the trick receives forty points for the first trick and thirty points for each trick thereafter.

If the contract was doubled, then the above scores double. If the contract was redoubled, then the scores quadruple. If the declarer wins a doubled contract, he receives an extra 50 points. If he wins a redoubled contract, he receives an extra 100 points.

Scoring Bonuses

If the contract was to win twelve tricks, this is known as a small slam and is worth extra points if achieved. If you complete a small slam while your team is vulnerable (having won one game in the rubber), you receive 750 bonus points. If your team is not vulnerable, you receive 500 bonus points.

If the contract was to win thirteen tricks, this is known as a grand slam and is worth extra points if achieved. If your team is vulnerable, you receive 1,500 bonus points. If your team is not vulnerable, you receive 1,000 bonus points.

The top five cards in the trump suit (ace, king, queen, jack, and ten) are called the honors. If you hold all five honors in your cards alone, you receive 150 bonus points. If you hold four honors in your cards alone, you receive 100 bonus points. If the contract is no trump and one player holds all four aces, he receives 150 bonus points.

If your team wins more tricks than you originally bid in your contract, each trick over the bid is called an overtrick. If the bid was not doubled or redoubled, your team receives the same number of points for each overtrick as for each regular trick as above. If the bid was doubled, your team receives 100 points for each overtrick if you were not vulnerable, or 200 points for each overtrick if you were vulnerable. If the bid was redoubled, your team receives 200 points for each overtrick if you were not vulnerable, or 400 points for each overtrick if you were vulnerable.

FACT

In the United States, the trump suits of clubs and diamonds are not as valuable as hearts and spades. Therefore, clubs and diamonds are called the minor suits and hearts and spades are called the major suits.

If your team does not win the number of tricks originally bid in your contract, neither side scores any points for the contract. Your opponents do receive a score based on the amount of tricks that were under your bid. If the bid was not doubled or redoubled, your opponents receive a score of fifty points for each undertrick (each trick less than what your contract was) if you were not vulnerable, or 100 points for each undertrick if you were vulnerable. If the bid was doubled and you were not vulnerable, your opponents receive a score of 100 points for the first undertrick, 200 points each for the second and third undertrick, and 300 points each for any further undertricks. If the bid was doubled and you were vulnerable, your opponents receive a score of 200 points for the first undertrick and 300 points each for any further undertricks. If the bid was redoubled, the points are double the doubled undertricks.

Scoring the Games

If you score 100 points or more below the line through winning contracts, you win that game. A new line is placed under these scores, and both teams start from zero. Any points that the losing team had below the line do not count toward the next game.

If your team wins the rubber, you receive a bonus of 700 points if you won two games in a row without your opponents winning any games. If your opponents win one of the games, and you win the rubber, your team only receives a bonus of 500 points. Now both columns are totaled and the team with the most points wins. The winning team subtracts the loser's score from their total score and divides by 100 to receive their "back door" score. Round up or down to get a whole number. The "back door" indicates the team's overall standing.

If you are unable to finish a rubber due to time constraints, and only one side has a game, that side scores 300 bonus points. If only one side has a part score, that side earns 100 bonus points.

Scoring Example

Scoring is even more complicated than bidding in bridge. The following is an illustration of scoring in contract bridge, with letters to annotate what each number means.

Sample Bridge Scoring Sheet	
We	**They**
	500 (g)
100 (e)	40 (f)
50 (b)	50 (d)
30 (a)	50 (c)
90 (a)	120 (c)
120 (e)	
	70 (f)
	120 (g)
390 (h)	950 (h)
	390 (h)
	560 (h)

(a) In the first hand of game one, We win the bid and have a contract of three hearts. We actually win ten tricks, completing the contract with one overtrick. We receive thirty points for each trick bid because the trump suit was hearts—thus receiving ninety points. This score is written below the line in the "We" column. We also receive thirty points for the overtrick, and this score is placed above the line in the "We" column. Because the total below the line is not 100 or more, a second hand is played.

(b) In the second hand, They win the bid with a contract of four clubs. They win only nine tricks and do not complete the contract. They receive no points, and We receive fifty points above the line for the one undertrick.

(c) In the third hand, They win the bid with a contract of three diamonds, and the bid is doubled. They win the nine tricks and complete the contract. They receive forty points for each trick bid because the trump suit is diamonds (twenty points) and the bid was doubled—thus receiving 120 points. They also win a bonus of 50 points above the line for fulfilling the doubled contract. They win this game and become vulnerable. A line is drawn beneath the scores to show the end of the first game, and a second game is played.

(d) In the first hand of the second game, We win the bid with a contract of two no trump. We only win seven tricks and do not complete the contract. We receive no points, and They receive fifty points for the undertrick because We are not vulnerable.

(e) In the second hand, We win the bid with a contract of four spades. We win the contract exactly, receiving 120 points under the line. We also held the four honors of A♠ K♠ Q♠ J♠ and receive 100 bonus points above the line. We win the second game, and now both teams are vulnerable.

(f) In the first hand of the third game, They win the bid with a contract of two no trump. They win nine tricks, completing the contract with one overtrick. They score seventy points below the line plus a forty-point bonus for the overtrick.

(g) In the second hand, They win the bid with a contract of four hearts. They complete the contract exactly, scoring 120 points below the line. This ends the rubber and They receive a 500-point bonus above the line for winning two games.

(h) Both sides are totaled, and then the loser's score is subtracted from the winner's score. This gives They a score of +6 Rubber (560/100 and rounded up to 6).

QUESTION?

May I win the game in one hand?
If a hand is doubled or redoubled, there are many ways to win in one hand. To win a game in only one hand with no doubles, a player must win a bid with at least three no trumps, four spades or hearts, or five clubs or diamonds.

Variations of Bridge

There are many variations that have been introduced to the game of bridge over the years. Chicago is a game that is complete in just four hands, so you can play with five or six players and rotate in the other player(s) much faster than when playing a rubber. Honeymoon Bridge is a game for two players, when you just can't seem to find another pair of partners who want to play when you do!

Chicago

Chicago originated at the Standard Club in Chicago. It is complete in four hands, with vulnerability being dictated based on which hand is being played. Chicago Bridge is played with four players forming two partnerships, using a standard pack of fifty-two cards. Aces are high, and twos are low. Chicago Bridge is dealt and played like contract bridge; the only difference is that the vulnerability changes with each hand, as follows:

- **Hand 1:** The dealer is North, and neither side is vulnerable.
- **Hand 2:** The dealer is East, and the dealer's team is vulnerable.
- **Hand 3:** The dealer is South, and the dealer's team is vulnerable.
- **Hand 4:** The dealer is West, and both sides are vulnerable.

Score for tricks, overtricks, undertricks, honors, bonuses, double, and redouble are played normally. Scores for tricks bid and made count toward game bonuses, with 300 points for a nonvulnerable game and 500 points for a vulnerable game. A part score on the fourth hand may reach game with a previous score. If it does not, the team gets a bonus of 100.

Honeymoon Bridge

Honeymoon Bridge is played with two players using a standard pack of fifty-two cards. The dealer deals thirteen cards, face down, one at a time to each player. The remaining cards are turned face down to form the stockpile.

The game begins with the dealer's opponent leading the first card. The dealer must follow suit if able. The winner of that trick takes the top card from the stockpile and the opponent takes the second card. The winner then leads the next trick. After the stockpile is depleted, a round of bidding occurs as in standard bridge. When bidding is complete, the declarer leads the first trick and the remaining tricks are played as before, only now a trump suit is involved if the contract contained a trump. Scoring is the same as in bridge.

Winning Strategies

In order to win at the game of bridge, you must understand and successfully play the bidding phase of the game. It is universally agreed upon that bidding is the most important part of bridge. You must make clear bids and bid correctly in order to allow you and your partner to complete the contracts and win.

Bidding allows you to show your partner the strength of your cards and what suits you hold. You can even signal whether you have any long suits and honor cards through a bidding system. You are not allowed to describe your hand through words, gestures, or facial expressions—so bidding is your only chance to give your partner clues. Of course, your partner must understand the communication in your bids in order to make proper responses.

FACT

Natural bids are those that convey the desire to play the contract with the specified trump and number of tricks. Artificial or conventional bids are those that have an agreed-upon meaning other than their actual bid. These meanings make up the bidding system for that team.

If you and your partner decide to use a bidding system to signal your hands, this system must be declared to the opponents before the game begins. If the system is complicated, you should write up a "convention card" and give that to your opponents for reference. This card contains all of the meanings and suggestions that you will be using in bidding. At the end of bidding, your opponents may also ask you about the bidding agreements that you used during the bid.

In creating a successful bid, the most basic method of natural bidding is the "point count system." This system requires you first to assign points to different areas, suits, and cards in your hand. First add up your high-card points (HCP) by counting four points for each ace, three points for each king, two points for each queen, and one point for each jack. Next, you'll add three points for each void you have in your hand (no cards of a particular suit), two points for only having a single card in one suit, and one point for only having two cards in one suit. Usually, a total of twenty-six points wins you the game, thirty-three points gives you a small slam, and thirty-seven points gives you a grand slam.

The common opening bids are the following:

- Thirteen or more points and five cards in a suit—open with that one and that suit.
- Thirteen to fifteen points but no five cards in a suit—open with one and the stronger minor suit.
- Fifteen to seventeen high-card points and no voids or single cards in one suit—open with one and no trump.

Some less common opening bids are the following:

- Twenty to twenty-four points and a balanced hand—open with two no trump.
- Twenty-five to twenty-seven points and a balanced hand—open with three no trump.
- Fewer than thirteen points but seven cards in one suit—open with three and that suit.
- Six cards in one suit with at least two honors—open with two and that suit.

If your partner has opened a hand with a one suit or no trump, you should only respond if you have six or more points in your hand. You should raise your partner's suit if you have four cards in the same suit, bid a different suit if you have four or more cards in that suit and you cannot support your partner's suit, or bid no trumps.

If you are going to overbid your opponent's bid, you should only bid a suit you have five or more cards in. You should have eight or more points to overbid at the one level, and at least eleven points to overbid at the two level. You should double your opponent's bid if you have ten or more points without five cards in one suit.

Chapter 10
All Fours

All Fours is a trick-taking game similar to whist and bridge, but it differs in the use of a unique scoring system that introduces complexity and a different strategy. There are many spinoffs and variances that have evolved from the game of All Fours, such as Cinch, Pinch, and Seven-Up. This chapter teaches you the structure behind the group of All Fours games, as well as the various differences and rules of play.

History of the Game

In pubs of seventeenth-century England, the game of All Fours was pioneered. The first recorded mention of the game is found in Charles Cotton's *The Complete Gamester.* According to Cotton, All Fours originated in Kent County. All Fours eventually traveled to the United States, where it gained in popularity in the nineteenth century. Many variations were derived from the game as players in various locations added their own rules and objectives. All Fours is still commonly played in England and Wales, and it recently has become popular in Trinidad. In the United States, All Fours survives in the game of Auction Pitch.

Playing All Fours

The objective of All Fours is to be the first team to score seven points by winning tricks containing the court cards and the high, low, and jack of the trump suit. Receiving the low point is luck of the deal, but scoring the remaining points requires you to play with some foresight. All Fours is usually played with four people forming two teams, with partners sitting across the table from one another. You'll need a standard pack of fifty-two cards, and aces are high, twos are low.

Determining the Trump Suit

All Fours opens with the each player cutting the deck, and the player with the highest value card deals first. When it's your turn to deal, deal out six cards, one at a time or in batches of three, face down to each player. Now turn up the next card to determine the trump suit. If the card is a jack, your team automatically scores one point for jack. The deal passes to the left for each hand.

Play begins with the player to the dealer's left (called the eldest hand) deciding if he's happy with the trump suit. If he is, he says, "I stand," and play begins. If he wants a different trump suit based on the cards in his hand, he says, "I beg." If you are the dealer and you prefer to keep the original trump suit, you respond, "Take one," and your opponents receive one point. If you agree that the trump should be changed, you say, "I run the cards" and deal three more cards to each player. You then turn up the next card to determine the trump suit and score one point if the card is a jack (as earlier). If the card is a new suit, play begins. If it is the same suit as the original trump suit, you'll deal three more cards to each player, and the process is repeated until a new suit is played or the deck of cards runs out. In that case the entire deck is shuffled and re-dealt.

In one variation of All Fours, if the card that is turned up is an ace, your team scores one point. If the card turned up is a six, your team scores two points. If the card turned up is a jack, your team scores three points.

Playing the Hand

After trump is determined, the player to the dealer's left leads the first trick by laying down one card face up on the table from his hand. Play continues to the left. When it's your turn, if the original card led was from the trump suit, you must follow suit if you can. If the original card was not from the trump suit, you must follow suit or play a trump card. If you can't do either of those, then you can play any remaining cards from your hand. The highest card in the suit led, or the highest trump, wins the trick, and that player leads the next trick. More tricks are played until everyone is out of cards.

Be warned! If you don't follow suit or throw a trump card, this counts as a revoke or renege, and you score penalty points. If it was a trump that was led, and you held one of the top five trump cards, your team loses fourteen points and the game is restarted. Otherwise you lose one point, and you cannot win a point for Game.

After the hand has been played, each team scores their hands (as mentioned following). The first team to reach seven points over multiple hands wins the game.

Scoring Games

All Fours games and variations are each scored using a unique method. This method carries across all of the All Fours games, although additional scores are sometimes added in. There are four specific scores. "High" awards one point if you hold the highest trump during play. "Low" awards one point if you held the lowest trump in your hand (not if you won the trick containing the lowest trump). "Jack" awards one point if you win a trick with the jack of trumps. If the jack was not dealt, no point is given. "Game" awards one point if your team contains the most valuable number of tricks.

In determining the highest tricks, aces of any suit are worth four points, kings are worth three points, queens are worth two points, jacks are worth one point, and tens are worth ten points. If both you and your opponent have the same number of trick points, neither of you wins the one Game point. When it's close to the end of a game, the points are counted in the order High, Low, Jack, and Game to determine who has reached seven first. This makes it impossible for the two teams to tie.

California Jack

California Jack is a game based on All Fours that uses the entire deck of cards and is played with only two players. The objective is to earn points by winning or losing tricks and receiving cards from the stockpile. You'll need a standard deck of fifty-two cards to play.

A random dealer is selected who deals out six cards, one at a time and face down, to each player. The remaining cards are turned face up in a stockpile, and the top card determines the trump suit. Deal then alternates with each hand.

If you are the dealer, play begins with the your opponent laying down one card from his hand. You must follow suit, if able, or you must play a trump if you have a card in the trump suit. Otherwise, you may play any card in your hand. The winner of the trick takes both cards and places them face down beside him. He then takes the top card from the stockpile to add to his hand. The loser of that trick takes the second card to add to his hand. Play continues until the stockpile is depleted, and each player then plays the remaining six cards in his hand.

The players score their hands and receive one point each for High, Low, Jack, and Game. The first player to ten points wins. If both players reach ten in the same hand, the points count in order of High, Low, Jack, and Game to avoid a tie.

Cinch

Also known as Double Pedro and High Five, Cinch is another game of the All Fours family and was a popular game before the introduction of bridge. Cinch is usually played with four players in teams of two, with partners sitting opposite one another. The objective of Cinch is to be the first team to reach fifty-one points. A standard pack of fifty-two cards is used. Aces are high, and twos are low, but the five that is the same color as the trump suit is also counted as a trump card, and the trump suit ranks as follows: ace, king, queen, jack, ten, nine, eight, seven, six, five, five again (same color as trump suit), four, three, and two.

FACT

The five of the trump suit is called the Right Pedro, and the five of the same color as the trump suit is called the Left Pedro. They are each worth five points each, bringing the total amount of possible points won up to fourteen.

Setup of Cinch

In Cinch, the players draw cards to determine their partners, the two highest playing against the two lowest. The highest card drawn determines the first dealer, who deals nine cards to each player in groups of three. The remaining cards are placed face down on the table to be used later on in the game.

After the deal, a round of bidding occurs. Each player has one chance to bid or pass, starting with the player to the dealer's left. If you choose to bid, you state the number of points that you believe your team can make within that hand. The minimum bid is one point, and the maximum bid is fourteen points. Each player may make a bid higher than the previous bid. The player with the highest bid names the trump suit without consulting his partner. If the first three players pass, the dealer may name the trump suit but is not obligated to take a minimum number of points.

Playing the Hand

Play starts with each player discarding a minimum of three cards, face up to the dealer. If a player discards more than three cards, the dealer then deals enough cards, face down, to bring the player's hand back up to six cards. You may not discard any trump cards unless you have more than six trumps in your hand. In that case, you may only discard three cards. When it is the dealer's turn to discard his cards, he may "rob the pack" and choose any cards out of the remaining stack that he wishes.

The player who made the highest bid leads the first trick by laying down any one card in his hand face up on the table. Play continues to the left, and when it's your turn, you must follow suit (if able) or lay down any other card in your hand. The highest card in the suit led, or the highest trump, wins the hand and that player leads the next trick. After all six tricks have been played, each team adds up the points collected in their hand for High, Low, Jack, Game, Right Pedro, and Left Pedro. If the high bidder's team scored the number of points bid, they win the difference in points between their hand and their opponent's hand. If they failed to score the number of points bid, the opponent's team scores the number of points that they collected, plus the original number of points that the high bidder's team bid. If the dealer selected a trump without a bid, the team with the most points scores the difference in their points and their opponents' points. The first team to fifty-one points wins the game.

ALERT!

Even if you're the high bidder and win the number of points bid, you might not win any points. For example, let's say the high bid was five points and that is all your team won, while your opponents won nine points. In this case, your opponents win four points (the difference between nine and five).

Pitch

Pitch is a North-American derivative of All Fours, with bidding added for an element of strategy. The objective of Pitch is for players to score points by winning tricks containing valuable cards. Pitch is typically played with four people forming two teams, with partners sitting across the table from one another. A standard pack of fifty-two cards is used. An enhanced version of Pitch can be played by adding a joker. The joker becomes the lowest card in play, but it does not count toward the point of Low. Low is given to the player who holds the lowest natural trump card. The joker counts as one extra point to the player who wins it in a trick, making the total available points five instead of four. The order of points scored is High, Low, Jack, Joker, and Game.

Bidding the Hand

Pitch opens with the players cutting the deck and the person who cuts the highest number deals first. The dealer deals six cards, three at a time, face down, to each player. Deal then passes to the left for each hand. You start off by going through one round of bidding where you can pass or bid on how many of High, Low, Jack, and Game points you will win during that hand (two, three or four).

When it's your turn, you may bid higher than the previous person or pass. The dealer can tie the highest bidder and win the bid. However, if you bid four, you are said to "smudge" and the dealer cannot take that bid from you. If the first three players pass, the dealer is forced to bid two. The highest bidder becomes the "pitcher" and pitches the trump suit by throwing his first card. The suit of that card is trump for that hand.

Playing the Tricks

Play begins with the pitcher leading the first trick. Play continues to the left and players must follow suit if they can, or play any other one card from their hand. The highest card in that suit led wins the trick and that player leads the next trick. If he leads a card from the trump suit, you must follow suit if you can. If he leads a card that is not from the trump suit, you may follow suit or play a trump card. If you can't follow suit or play a trump, you can play any of the remaining cards in your hand. The highest card in the suit led, or the highest trump, wins the trick, and that player leads the next trick. This continues until all of the players are out of cards.

FACT

Variations of the total points needed to win Pitch include playing to seven points or eleven points. It's up to you and your opponents to decide the length of the game and the amount of time you all want to play!

After the trick is over, you view your cards to see who won High, Low, Jack, and Game (and Joker, if you're playing that variation). If your team had the high bid and scored that many points, you score the number of points that you won (i.e., if you bid two and won three points, you receive three points). If you do not make the bid, you lose points equal to the number that you bid. If you're the first team to twenty-one points, on a hand that you won the bid, you win the game. If you reach twenty-one points but did not make the bid, you must continue playing hands until you do win a bid, giving your opponents a chance to catch up and win.

All Fives

All Fives is another All Fours derivative where points are also scored for each of the trump cards used to make the point of Game. The objective of All Fives is for players to score points by winning tricks containing court cards. All Fives is typically played with two or three people playing individually or with four people playing in partnerships. A standard pack of fifty-two cards is used. Aces are high, and twos are low.

Rules of Play

A random dealer is selected and deals out six cards, one at a time or in batches of three, face down, to each player. The dealer turns up the next card to determine the trump suit. If the card is a jack, the dealer scores one point for Jack. The deal passes to the left for each hand.

Play begins with the player to the dealer's left deciding if he's happy with the trump suit, based on the cards in his hand. If he is, he says, "I stand," and play begins. If he wants a different trump suit, he says, "I beg." If you are the dealer, and you prefer to keep the trump suit as the card you turned up, you respond, "Take one," and give your opponents one point. If you agree and want a new trump suit, you say, "I run the cards," and deal three more cards to each player. You turn up the next card, and if it's a new suit, play begins. If it is the same suit as the original trump suit, you deal three more cards to each player and continue the process until a new suit is played or the deck of cards runs out.

After trump is determined, the player to the dealer's left leads the first trick by laying down one card face up on the table from his hand. Play continues to the left. When it's your turn, if the original card led was from the trump suit, you must follow suit if you can. If the original card was not from the trump suit, you must follow suit or play a trump card. If you can't follow suit or trump, you can play any of the other cards in your hand. The highest card in the suit led, or the highest trump, wins the trick and that player leads the next trick. This continues until all of the players are out of cards.

Scoring All Fives

All Fives is best scored using a cribbage board. While playing, as you win tricks with various trump cards, you automatically receive points as follows: the ace scores you four points, the king scores you three points, the queen scores you two points, the jack scores you one point, the ten scores you ten points, and the five scores you five points. After the game is over, you all view your cards to see who won High, Low, and Game. The first player or team to earn sixty-one points wins the game. On a cribbage board, that will be the first team to cycle around the board once and pass the starting line. If you're playing with three players, you should each take one column and go up and back down that same column, or keep track with paper instead.

Chapter 11
Euchre

E uchre is another popular trick-taking game that is played with multiple players in a group setting. Euchre uses a smaller deck of cards than the standard deck of fifty-two, making play a bit speedier. There are multiple variations that have been introduced in the development and expansion of euchre. This chapter will introduce you to this group of euchre games.

History of the Game

Euchre is a classic card game with a disputed history. There are arguments that euchre is a descendant of the Spanish game Triumph, the German game Jucker, the French game Triomphe, or the game Ecarte that was popularized by the Pennsylvania Dutch. Regardless of its origins, euchre was very popular in Europe during the eighteenth and nineteenth centuries and found its way to the United States in the early nineteenth century. Euchre remains very popular in the U.S. Navy, and in fact may have been initiated in the United States and other countries through this venue. Euchre was the game of choice until bridge appeared on the scene and gained more popularity.

North American Euchre

The North American version of euchre is a popular game in Canada and the Northeast and Midwest in the United States. It was first introduced in New Orleans and spread north along the Mississippi River, where the modern version is played today. You'll need four players divided into two teams, with partners sitting opposite one another. You'll also need a shortened deck of twenty-four cards consisting of the ace, king, queen, jack, ten, and nine of each suit. The trump suit, chosen later in the game, has seven cards ranking from high to low as: Right Bower (jack of the trump suit), Left Bower (jack of the same color as the trump suit), ace, king, queen, ten, and nine. The cards in each of the other suits (except the jack of the same color as the trump suit) rank as normal.

Players try to win at least three of the five tricks in the hand, earning points for their team. The first team to score ten wins the game.

Dealing

The first dealer is selected by cutting the deck. The player who receives the highest card is the first dealer. The deal then rotates clockwise as each hand is played. The dealer deals the deck clockwise, giving each player a group of two or three cards face down in any order. He then deals clockwise again, giving any player who was dealt two cards in the first round three cards in the second, and vice versa. The next card is turned face up, and this up card is used to determine the trump suit. The last three cards are left face down and are not used.

FACT

Euchre is played with a shortened deck of cards, but just how many cards to play with is often disputed. Some players play with twenty-four cards, some with thirty-two cards, and some with thirty-six cards. Play remains the same; it just changes the number of tricks that have to be played out.

Selecting the Trump

After deal, it's time to determine the trump suit. The player to the dealer's left may choose to accept the up-card suit as the trump, or she can pass. If she passes, the next person may choose to pass or accept the trump. This continues around the table until the trump is selected or the dealer passes.

The correct terminology in accepting trump is to say, "I order it up," followed by the dealer's partner agreeing, "I assist." If you don't want the card that was turned up as the trump suit, you say, "I pass."

If the up card is selected as trump, the dealer picks up the up card and adds it to his hand, discarding one card face down, and you begin playing tricks. If all players pass on the up card, it is turned face down. Players then have the option to make any suit trump, other than the up-card suit. This starts with the player to the dealer's left, who may either declare a suit or pass. If all players pass during the second round, the cards are thrown in, and the next player deals. If one player chooses a trump suit, play will begin. That player's team becomes the "makers," and the opposite side becomes the "defenders." If you choose as trump the suit of the same color as the original turned-up trump, it is called "making it next." If you choose as trump either of the suits opposite of the original turned-up card, it is called "crossing it."

Playing the Tricks

Play begins with the player to the dealer's left laying his first card face up on the table, choosing any one card in his hand. Play continues clockwise. When it's your turn, you must follow suit, if you can, by playing a card of the same suit that was led. If you cannot follow suit, you may play any one card in your hand. The trick is won by whoever played the highest card of the suit led unless a trump was played, in which case the highest trump wins. The winner of each trick leads the next one.

FACT

In euchre terminology, "the Dutchman" is when you hold both bowers (both the trump jack and the jack of the same color as the trump) and the ace of trump. "Dutchman's Point" is the point you win when holding these cards.

After all tricks have been played, the hand is scored. If your team is the makers and you win three or four tricks, you score one point. If you win all five tricks, you score two points. If you take fewer than three tricks, you are "euchred," and your opponents, the defenders, score two points. The game is normally played until one team reaches ten points.

British Euchre

British euchre includes the introduction of the Benny card as high trump, for added complexity. This is another game played with four players divided into two teams with partners sitting opposite one another. You'll need a pack of twenty-five cards consisting of the ace, king, queen, jack, ten, and nine in each suit and an additional Benny card, which is either a joker or 2♠. The trump suit has eight cards ranking from high to low as: Benny, Right Bower (jack of the trump suit), Left Bower (jack of the same color as the trump suit), ace, king, queen, ten, and nine. Each of the other suits has five or six cards ranking as normal. The goal in each hand is to win at least three of the five tricks in the hand, earning your team points. The team that scores ten or more points wins the game.

Dealing the Hand

The first dealer is selected through a process where you each cut the deck. If you cut the highest card, you become the dealer, and the deal rotates clockwise after each hand is played. You deal the deck clockwise, giving each player a group of two or three cards face down in any order. You then deal clockwise again, giving any player who was dealt two cards in the first round three cards in the second, and vice versa. You turn up the next card in the pack face up and this up card is used as a basis for selecting the trump suit. The last four cards are left face down and are not used.

Picking the Trump Suit

After dealing, it's time to pick the trump suit. If the Benny is turned up and you're the dealer, your team automatically becomes the makers. You must choose the trump suit before looking at your cards. You then pick up the Benny and discard a card from your hand. If the Benny is not turned up, the player to your left may choose to accept the up-card suit as the trump, accept the suit as trump and "go alone," or she can pass. Choosing to go alone means that the player's partner does not play in this hand. This continues around the table until the trump is selected or the dealer passes.

If the up card is selected as trump, you (as the dealer) pick up the up card and add it to your hand, discarding one card face down, and begin playing tricks. If all four players pass on the up card, it is turned face down. The players then have the option to make any suit trump, other than the up-card suit. Starting with the player to the dealer's left, each player can pass or name a trump. If you all pass during the second round, the cards are thrown in and the next player deals. If a trump suit is selected, that player's team becomes the "makers" and the opposite side becomes the "defenders." At this point any of the other players may choose to "go alone" as well.

Playing the Tricks

If all four players are in the game, the play begins with the player to the dealer's left laying his first card. If one player is playing alone, the person to that player's left leads first. If two players are playing alone, the defender leads.

The first player to lead may lay down any one card in his hand face up on the table. Play continues clockwise around the table. When it's your turn, you must follow suit, if you can, by playing one card of the same suit that was led. If you cannot follow suit, you may play any card. The trick goes to the player who played the highest card of the suit led, unless a trump was played, in which case the highest trump wins. The winner of each trick starts off the next one.

QUESTION?

What does Bower mean?
Bower is derived from the German word *Bauer*, which means a farmer or peasant and is also a word for the jack. Through the years, the third-highest-ranking card has been called a knave, a jack, a Bauer, and a chevalier.

After all tricks have been played, the hand is scored. If your team is the makers, you score one point if you win three or four tricks. You score two points if you win all five tricks (four points if one player of your team is going alone). If you take fewer than three tricks, you are "euchred," and the defenders score two points (four points if one of the defender's team is going alone). The game is normally played to five, seven, ten, or eleven points.

Bid Euchre

Bid euchre introduces an element of bidding in which you dictate the number of tricks you are attempting to take in that hand. You'll typically play with four players forming two teams with partners sitting opposite one another. In this section you'll see rules of play for using two decks of twenty-four cards each, consisting of the ace, king, queen, jack, ten, and nine of each suit. You can also play with just one deck of thirty-two or thirty-six cards and vary the minimum or maximum bid. The trump suit has eight cards ranking from high to low as: Benny, Right Bower (jack of the trump suit), Left Bower (jack of the same color as the trump suit), ace, king, queen, ten, and nine. Each of the other suits has five or six cards ranking as normal. There will be two of each card since two decks are used. The objective in each hand is for you to bid the correct number of tricks and win that amount or more.

Bidding the Hand

The first dealer is selected at random and deals the entire deck clockwise. You each have one opportunity to bid, starting with the player on the dealer's left. You bid by naming a number of tricks plus the trump suit you wish to have, or no trumps (e.g., "four, hearts" or "five, no trump"). When it's your turn, you can pass or bid an amount higher than the previous bid. The player with the highest bid becomes the declarer, and the suit named in the bid becomes trump. The minimum bid is three tricks, and if the first three players do not bid, the dealer must bid three tricks and call a trump suit.

Playing the Tricks

The high bidder lays his first trick by playing any one card out of his hand face up on the table. Play continues clockwise around the table. When it's your turn, you must follow suit, if you can, by playing one card of the same suit that was led. If you cannot follow suit, you may play any card in your hand. The trick is won by whoever played the highest card of the suit led or the highest trump if a trump was played. If you're the first to lay one of two identical cards in the same trick, your card beats the second player to lay down. The winner of each trick starts off the next one.

If you are the declarer, and your team wins the number of tricks you bid, or more, you win one point for each trick won. If you do not win the number of tricks bid, you lose points equal to the amount of your bid. Your opponents score one point for each trick they won, regardless of whether your team won or lost the hand. The game is won when one team reaches the agreed-upon score (usually thirty-two points) in a hand in which they are the high bidder.

The Game of 500

The game 500 gets its name because the first team to reach 500 points wins the game. It's is the national card game of Australia, although it was invented in the United States and the rules were copyrighted in 1904 by the U.S. Playing Card Company. The game is played with four players divided into two teams with partners sitting opposite one another. The objective in each hand is to win 500 points through capturing tricks. A pack of forty-three cards is used, consisting of the ace, king, queen, jack, ten, nine, eight, seven, six, five, and four of hearts and diamonds, and the ace, king, queen, jack, ten, nine, eight, seven, six, and five of clubs and spades, and one joker. The trump suit has cards ranking from high to low as follows: joker, Right Bower (jack of the trump suit), Left Bower (jack of the same color as the trump suit), ace, king, queen, jack, ten, nine, eight, seven, six, five, and four if it's a red suit. Each of the other suits has cards ranking as normal with ace as high down to five or four.

A Round of Bidding

The first dealer is selected at random and deals ten cards to each player in a clockwise direction. Each player is dealt a batch of three cards, then one to the kitty, a batch of four cards to each player, one to the kitty, a batch of three cards to each player, and a last card to the kitty. Deal continues to the player on the left with each hand.

A round of bidding begins with the player to the dealer's left. When it's your turn, you may pass, bid a number of tricks and a trump suit, bid a number of tricks and no trump, bid Misere, or bid Open Misere. If you bid a number, this is the number of tricks you believe you and your partner can take. The minimum bid is six. If you bid Misere, or Nullo, you believe you can lose all of the tricks with your partner out of play. If you bid Open Misere, you believe that you can lose all of the tricks with your cards showing to your opponents.

If each player passes, the cards are thrown in and the next player deals. If one player bids, the next player must pass or bid higher by bidding more tricks or a higher suit. The suits rank in order from low to high as spades, clubs, diamonds, hearts, and no trump. As an example, you can bid seven hearts and the next player can bid seven no trump or eight spades to outbid you. Misere can only be bid after a player bids a seven, and is beaten by a player who bids an eight. Open Misere can be bid at any time, but is beaten by a 10♥ or higher.

Bid continues around the table until the other three players pass. If you pass, you cannot bid at any further point in the bidding round. The highest bid becomes the contract, the high bidder becomes the contractor, and the suit named becomes trump.

ALERT!

The majority of euchre games can add a fifth player by adding this partner rule. The high bidder becomes partners with the player who holds the best card in the trump suit. The partner is silent until he can play that card.

Playing the Tricks

If you won the bid and are the contractor, you start by picking up the cards in the kitty. You must then discard three cards, using any combination of cards from your hand and the kitty. If your contract is Misere or Open Misere, your partner does not participate in the hand.

You start playing the tricks by laying your first card. You may play any one card in your hand. If you are playing Open Misere, you must then turn up your entire hand for your opponents to see. Play continues clockwise around the table. Each player must follow suit if he can, by playing a card of the same suit that you led. If a player cannot follow suit, he may play any card. The trick is won by whoever played the highest card of the suit led, or the highest trump played if the bid contained a trump suit. The winner of each trick leads to the next one.

If the hand is being played with trump, the joker is the highest card in that suit. If there is no trump, or the contract is Misere or Open Misere, the contractor can determine what suit the joker is (if he holds it) and the joker becomes the highest card in that suit. If the contractor does not hold the joker, it becomes the highest suit in the hand, but can only be played when you have no other cards in the suit led.

Scoring the Game

After all the cards have been played, the contract is scored according to the chart shown here.

Scoring of 500					
Tricks	Spades	Clubs	Diamonds	Hearts	No Trumps
Six	40	60	80	100	120
Seven	140	160	180	200	220
Eight	240	260	280	300	320
Nine	340	360	380	400	420
Ten	440	460	480	500	520

A bid of Misere is worth 250 points, and a bid of Open Misere is worth 500 points.

If you are the contractor, your team scores your contract as above, with no bonuses for extra tricks won. If you win all of the tricks, this is considered a slam, and you win a minimum of 250 points. Your opponents receive ten points for each trick they won.

If your team does not take as many tricks as you bid, or takes a trick in Misere or Open Misere, you lose the number of points equal to your bid. Your opponents still receive ten points for each trick they won.

The first team to reach 500 points on a contract that they bid wins the game. If either team scores negative 500 points, they automatically lose the game.

If you are the contractor and bid fewer than eight spades and win a slam, you receive 250 points. If you bid higher than eight clubs, you receive the number of points equal to your contract in the table.

Spoil Five

Spoil Five is part of the euchre family and is often regarded as the national card game of Ireland. The game can be played with two to ten players but is typically played with four or five people. The objective of Spoil Five is to try to win enough tricks to win the pool. This game does not use a shortened deck; instead, the entire deck of fifty-two cards is used. The highest trumps are the five of that suit, the jack of that suit, and then the A♥. The rest of the cards in the trump suit rank (from high to low) as ace, king, queen, and then if the trump suit color is black, the rank is two, three, four, six, seven, eight, nine, and ten. If the trump suit color is red, it ranks ten, nine, eight, seven, six, four, three, and two.

Therefore, the rank in the trump suit from high to low is like so:

♥ 5 J A K Q 10 9 8 7 6 4 3 2

♦ 5 J A♥ A K Q 10 9 8 7 6 4 3 2

♣ 5 J A♥ A K Q 2 3 4 6 7 8 9 10

♠ 5 J A♥ A K Q 2 3 4 6 7 8 9 10

The nontrump suits rank from high to low as follows:

♥ K Q J 10 9 8 7 6 5 4 3 2

♦ K Q J 10 9 8 7 6 5 4 3 2 A

♣ K Q J A 2 3 4 5 6 7 8 9 10

♠ K Q J A 2 3 4 5 6 7 8 9 10

Dealing the Hand

Spoil Five opens with each player anteing two or three coins to the pool, depending on how you choose to play the game. If you are the dealer, you deal five cards, face down, to each player in groups of two and three, or three and two. You then turn up the next card, and the suit of that card becomes trump. If the turned-up card is an ace, you may "rob the card" by adding it to your hand and discarding a card. If any other player has been dealt the ace of the trump suit, he may rob the card by taking the turned-up trump before playing his first card and discarding a card in his hand.

Playing the Tricks

Play begins with the player to the dealer's left leading the first trick by laying down any one card from his hand face up on the table. Play continues clockwise around the table. If a trump is led and you have a trump, you must follow suit. If a nontrump suit is led, you may play any card from your hand. This is where 500 differs from most games—you do not have to follow suit, even if you're able to. The highest card of the suit led, or the highest trump if trumps are played, wins the trick. The winner of the trick leads the next one until all five tricks have been played.

The three highest trumps (5, jack, A♥) have the privilege of reneging when a lower trump is led. This means that if a trump is led, and you only have one of the three high trumps, you are not required to play it. You can play a nontrump instead.

If a player wins three tricks, he takes the pool. If no player wins three tricks, the pool is carried forward, and each player but the dealer adds a coin to it.

If a player wins the first three tricks, he may either collect the pool, in which case a new hand is dealt, or he may call "jinx" and lead to a fourth hand. This means that he is attempting to win five hands. If he does, each player must pay him an additional amount. If he doesn't win all five hands, the pool carries forward.

Chapter 12

Rummy

The earliest form of the game rummy can be traced back to the Mexican game of Conquian, played in the nineteenth century. Rummy is one of the most popular draw-and-discard games because of its fast-paced action and simple rules. It encompasses a large variety of games, and this chapter will show you the rules behind rummy, gin rummy, Manipulation Rummy, and Rummy 500.

The Meld

A meld is a collection of cards. There are two types of melds—groups of cards and sequences of cards. A group of three of a kind or four of a kind makes up a group, such as 5♠ 5♥ 5♦. A sequence of cards is actually a run of three or more cards within the same suit, such as 4♣ 5♣ 6♣. A king and ace are not consecutive cards in a sequence, but an ace and a two are. A card can only belong to one meld at a time. You cannot use the same card in a sequence and in a group.

FACT

When the game is over, any cards that are in your hand that are not part of a meld are called "deadwoods." These deadwoods give you penalty points based on their values, so you'll want to form melds as quickly as possible or get rid of high-value deadwood cards.

Standard Rummy

The standard game of rummy is played with two to six players using a deck of fifty-two cards. All of the court cards are worth ten points each, and the numbered cards are worth their face value. An ace is worth one point. While playing rummy, you try to dispose of all of the cards in your hand through the formation of multiple melds.

Dealing

A random dealer is chosen and deals out the cards, one at a time, face down, to each player. If there are two players, each player receives ten cards. If there are three or four players, each player is dealt seven cards. If there are five or six players, each player receives six cards. The dealer turns up the next card, face up, and this begins the discard pile. The remainder of the cards are placed face down next to the discard pile and become the stockpile. Deal continues to alternate after each game.

Completing a Turn

The game starts with the player to the dealer's left completing a turn. When it's your turn, you must first choose to draw the top card on the discard pile or the top card of the stockpile. You add the card you drew to your hand. If you have a meld, you may lay it down on the table (although you are not obligated to do so). You may only lay down one meld per turn. You may also choose to lay off other cards on your opponent's melds or previous melds that you have laid down, by adding cards to continue a sequence of cards, or add a card to a group of three. After you have laid down as many cards as you choose, your next step is to discard a card. This card is placed face up on top of the discard pile. If you drew the top card from the discard pile, you may not discard that same card within the same turn. The next player to the left completes a turn, and play continues multiple times around the table.

If the stockpile runs out of cards, and the next player does not want to take the top card on the discard pile, the discard pile is turned over to form a new stockpile and play continues.

Game Over

Play for that hand ends when the first player discards his last card by melding, laying off, or discarding his last card. The other players then add up the values of the cards still in their hand. Those points are added to the winner's score. More hands are dealt until a player wins by reaching a specific number of points (agreed upon before play began) or until a specific number of hands have been played (agreed upon before play began). The player with the highest score at that time wins the game.

Once a player discards his final card and the game is over, you may not discard cards from your hand to get rid of penalty points, even if they are melds or if you can play the cards on existing melds on the table. Sorry, those are the rules!

Variations

There are many variations to the game of rummy. You may play more than one meld in a turn, but you may not lay off on your opponent's melds until you have laid down a meld of your own. If you go out without having laid down any melds or without laying off cards to your opponent's hands, you receive a bonus of ten points or your score for that hand is doubled, depending on how you and the other players have chosen to play the game.

In one variation, you must discard your final card to go out. If you lay down all of your cards in melds or on your opponent's cards, you must wait until the next turn and draw a card from the stockpile. If you can play that card, you must do so and wait another turn. If you can discard that card, the game is over, and you win.

A scoring variation is that you receive points equal to the value of your hand when another player goes out. When the first person reaches 100 points, the player with the fewest points wins.

Gin Rummy

Gin rummy is more complicated than standard rummy because a player cannot lay down melds during play. You must hold your cards in your hand until you can go out, so you do not have the option of playing off your previous melds or your opponent's melds to assist you in discarding your cards. Gin rummy is played with only two players using a standard pack of fifty-two cards. All face cards are worth ten points, and the numbered cards are worth their face value. An ace is worth one point. Each player tries to arrange the cards in his hand into melds to go out first.

Rules of Play

A random dealer is chosen and deals out ten cards, one at a time, face down to each player. The dealer turns up the next card, face up, and this begins the discard pile. The remainder of the cards are placed face down next to the discard pile and become the stockpile. Deal continues to alternate after each game.

Play begins with the dealer's opponent choosing to take the card in the discard pile or passing it. If he passes, the dealer has a chance to draw the card. If the dealer also passes on taking the card, the opponent starts a normal turn by drawing a card from the stockpile and discarding a card to the waste pile. From that point on, on each turn you can choose to draw the top card on the discard pile or the top card of the stockpile. The advantage of taking from the discard pile is that because the card is face up, you know what card you are choosing. Of course, if that card does not work toward building a meld with any other cards in your hand, you are better off drawing from the stockpile. You add the card you drew to your hand. The next step is to discard a card. This card is placed face up on top of the discard pile. If you drew the top card from the discard pile, you may not discard that same card within the same turn.

Knocking

Play ends when a player knocks on the table. Knocking can occur during any turn, immediately after the player picks up his card, if the player can form enough melds. Once you knock, you discard one card and spread the rest of your hand on the table, face up. You then arrange your cards into their various melds and deadwood.

In order to knock, the total value of your deadwood cards must be less than ten. If you are able to form melds with the majority of your cards, but have a deadwood value of more than ten, you must rearrange your melds or wait for different cards. Knocking with zero deadwood cards is known as gin and receives a bonus.

Your opponent then turns over his cards, face up, and arranges them into melds if possible. If you did not go gin (by discarding all of your cards with no deadwoods), your opponent may play any of his deadwood cards off your melds. As an example, if you had a meld of 6♥ 7♥ 8♥, your opponent may play a 5♥ or 9♥ on your meld. If you did go gin, your opponent may lay down his melds, but may not play any deadwood cards on your melds.

You are not forced to knock, even if you are able. You may continue to play in the hopes of obtaining a better score. Play also ends if the stockpile is reduced to two cards. The hand is then over, and neither player scores points for that deal.

Scoring the Game

Each player adds up the value of his deadwood cards. If the knocker's count is lower than his opponent's, he scores the difference between the two hands. If the knocker did not go gin, and the count of their hands is equal, or if the knocker's count is higher than his opponent's, the knocker has been undercut. If this happens, the opponent scores the difference between the two hands and a bonus of ten points. If the knocker goes gin, he receives a bonus of twenty points.

A player who goes gin can never be undercut. Even if the other player has no deadwood cards, the knocker gets the bonus of twenty points, and her opponent scores zero points.

The game continues with more hands until you or your opponent reaches 100 points. That player receives a bonus of 100 points. If the winner's opponent did not score any points, he receives another bonus of 100 points (for a total of 200 bonus points). Each player also receives a "line bonus" of 20 points for each hand that he won. The player with the most points wins and is typically paid the difference between his points and his opponent's points.

Variations

There are multiple variations of gin rummy. A two-player variation is that the dealer deals eleven cards to his opponent, and the game begins with the opponent discarding his first card. A scoring variation is that going gin receives a bonus of twenty-five points, and an undercut receives a bonus of twenty points. If three players wish to play, the dealer deals to the other two players and does not play. The loser of that hand deals next (therefore the first dealer and the winner play the next hand). If four players wish to play, the game is played with two teams. In each hand, one of the players plays one of the opponents. Players alternate their opponents, but stay in the same teams. The team that scores 125 points first wins the game.

Manipulation Rummy

Also known as Carousel, Shanghai, Rummi, or the tile game Rummikub, Manipulation Rummy allows a player to manipulate the cards on the table to form new melds so that he can play more cards from his hand. The objective of Manipulation Rummy is to try to meld all of your cards onto the table using the cards in your hand, your previous melds, and your opponent's melds. The game requires three to five players and two standard decks of fifty-two cards. Aces are considered high and cannot be melded into a sequence with low cards.

Rules of Play

The game starts by choosing a random dealer who shuffles the cards and deals seven cards, face down, one at a time to each player. The remaining cards are turned face down and placed in the middle of the table to form the stockpile. Play begins with the player to the left of the dealer. If you are able to meld any of your cards onto the table, you must do so. If you can't meld any cards, you must draw cards from the stockpile until you can. A meld can be a sequence of three cards in the same suit, or a three-of-a-kind. There is no initial draw and no discard in the game of Manipulation Rummy.

FACT

A three-of-a-kind must consist of three cards of different suits. 4♣ 4♠ 4♥ is valid, but 4♣ 4♥ 4♥ is not. If you have two of the exact same cards, you'll need to create another group of cards or play the other card in a sequence.

Play continues clockwise around the table. After an initial meld has been laid down, you can manipulate the cards that have been melded on the table in order to create new melds using at least one card in your hand. For example, if there is a meld of 4♣ 5♣ 6♣ on the table and a meld of 7♣ 7♥ 7♠, you may lay down the 7♦ from your hand, move the 7♣ over to the sequence and add an 8♣ from your hand. The new melds would be 4♣ 5♣ 6♣ 7♣ 8♣ and 7♦ 7♥ 7♠. If you do rearrange the melds on the table, when you are finished each card on the table must still be part of a legal meld. The first player to get rid of all the cards in his hand wins that hand.

Scoring

If you are not the player to get rid of your cards first, you receive penalty points for the cards remaining in your hand. Cards with a value below ten receive five points each, tens and face cards receive ten points each, and aces are worth fifteen points each. The game is played to a specified number, determined before play begins (usually 200 or 300 points), and when one player goes over that number, the player with the fewest points wins the game.

Variations

There are similar games and multiple variations of Manipulation Rummy. In the game of Shanghai, each player is dealt ten cards, and the rest of the game is played like Manipulation Rummy. The only difference is that you are not required to lay off all of your melds if you have more than one. This allows you to play one meld at a time and not have to draw new cards. If you manipulate existing melds, it is called a Shanghai. Players receive one point for each card left in their hand after the first player melds all of his cards.

The game of Carousel is played with two decks of cards and two jokers. On your turn, you must pick up one card from the stockpile and then meld if you can. If you cannot, you draw a second card and then meld if you can. If you still cannot, you draw a third card and play passes to the next player. If you lay down a joker, another player may replace the joker with the correct card and then use the joker elsewhere on the table to form a new meld. This must happen within the same turn as replacing the joker.

The game of Rummikub uses colored tiles instead of cards with suits and also uses two jokers. If you cannot meld on your turn, you only pick up one tile from the stock available, and you cannot play it until your next turn. In order to initially lay down melds, the total value of the tiles you lay down must equal a minimum of thirty points. If you lay down a joker, another player may replace the joker with the correct tile and then use the joker elsewhere on the table to form a new meld.

FACT

Rummikub was developed by the late Mr. Ephraim Hertzano in the early 1930s. The first Rummikub sets were handmade one at a time in the Hertzano backyard by his family. Today Rummikub is the third bestselling game in the world!

Rummy 500

Also known as 500 Rummy or 500 Rum, this game of rummy allows for some very large hands and a chance to score a lot of points. Rummy 500 is played with two or more players using a standard pack of fifty-two cards. All face cards are worth ten points, and the numbered cards are worth their face value. An ace is worth one point if played in a sequence, or fifteen points if played in a group or left in the player's hand. If playing with jokers, they are worth fifteen points each. The objective of Rummy 500 is to have the fewest points when one player reaches the cut-off score.

Rules of Play

A random dealer is chosen who deals out the cards, one at a time, face down, to each player. If there are two players, each player receives thirteen cards. If there are three or more players, each player is dealt seven cards. The dealer turns up the next card, face up, and this begins the discard pile. The remainder of the cards are placed face down next to the discard pile and become the stockpile. Deal continues to alternate after each game.

Play begins with the player to the dealer's left completing a turn. Each turn requires the player to draw the top card on the discard pile, the top card of the stockpile, or a card farther down the discard pile (but only if he can meld that card with other cards in his hand) and lay them down. If you choose the card farther down the discard pile, you must add the other cards above into your hand. Whatever card(s) you choose to take, if you have a meld, you may lay it down on the table (although you are not obligated to do so). You may also choose to lay off other cards on your opponent's melds or previous melds that you have laid down. When you lay off on your opponent's cards, do not actually add the cards to his hand. Place them in front of you so you can score points for them later.

FACT

To properly draw a card under the top card of the discard pile, you should first show how you'll meld the card you're drawing, pick up all the cards from the discard pile, meld that bottom card, and add the remaining cards to your hand.

After you are done laying down cards (or if you choose not to lay down any cards), you end your turn by discarding a card. This card is placed face up on top of the discard pile, but slightly to the side of the card beneath it so that all cards are fanned out and visible. If you drew the top card from the discard pile, you may not discard that same card within the same turn. Play continues clockwise multiple times around the table.

Game Over

Play for that hand ends when the stockpile runs out of cards or when the first player discards his last card by melding, laying off, or discarding his last card. No other players may discard cards from their hands, even if they have melds or could lay off on other melds.

After a player goes out, the other players add up the value of the cards in their hands and subtract that from the value of the cards they have laid on the table. Hands continue to be dealt until a player's cumulative score reaches 500 points with two people playing; 300 points with three people; 250 points with four or five people; or 200 points with six to eight people. The player with the most points at that stage wins.

Variations

Variations of Rummy 500 include all of the variations for rummy and a couple new options. A joker may be used as a wild card, but once it is melded it must continue to be used as that specific card. If a player goes out on his first turn, he scores twice as much for his melds. If a player takes the entire discard pile, he does not have to meld the bottom card. If a player discards a card that is easily melded, another player may yell "Rummy!" and play the card. If a player leaves a card lower down in the discard pile that could easily be melded, another player out of turn may yell "Rummy!" and pick up the pile of cards, meld the bottom card, and add the remaining cards to his hand. Another variation gives cards values of five (for ace through nine), ten (for ten and face cards), and fifteen for ace and joker.

Other Rummy Variations

There are many other rummy variations than the ones previously described, but they are very similar to these rummy games, build upon these games, or are just much less commonly seen.

Conquian

Conquian is actually the earliest known rummy game in the Western world. It is played with forty cards (remove the eights, nines, and tens from a standard pack of cards). The game is played with two players, who are each dealt ten cards. The first player can choose to take the initial discard or pass, allowing the dealer to take it. If the dealer passes, regular play begins. In each turn, you can pick up the card in the discard pile, but only if you can use it to make a meld on the table. If you cannot, you turn the discard face down in a second discard pile, pick up the first card in the stockpile, and turn it over on top of the initial discard pile. You may then pick up this card, but again, only if you can use it to make a meld on the table. If you cannot, you leave it for your opponent and your turn is over. If you pick up a card and make a meld, you may also play off other melds or add other melds that you have in your hand. You then discard, and your turn is over.

In Conquian, your opponent also has the option of forcing you to pick up the face-up card from the discard pile and meld it with cards on the table (only if the cards actually meld). You cannot refuse this play!

Oklahoma Gin

Oklahoma Gin is extremely similar to, and builds upon, gin rummy. The major difference is that the first card that is turned up and starts the discard pile determines the maximum number of points that the player can have in his deadwood cards when he knocks. A face card is valued at ten, and the number cards correspond to their numerical value. If an ace is turned up, the player may only knock if he can go gin. Another difference lies in the determination of points at the end of a hand. If the card turned face-up to start the discard pile is a spade, the final score for that deal is doubled. The target score is 150 points.

Kaluki

Also known as Kalookie, Kalooki, and Kaloochie, this game is played with two decks of cards and four jokers. Fifteen cards are dealt if there are two, three, or four players. Thirteen cards are dealt if there are five players, and eleven cards are dealt for six players. A meld may not contain duplicate cards (for example, a three-of-a-kind meld may not consist of 6♥ 6♥ 6♠). The ace can count in sequence with a king and queen. Until you lay down your own first meld, you may not play on others' melds, and you may only pick up cards from the stockpile. The exception to this is if you are laying down your initial meld on that turn. You may remove a joker from the table, replace it with the card it represents, and add the joker to your hand for play at a later time. In scoring a hand, unplayed jokers count as twenty-five points, jokers on the table count as the card they represent, aces count as eleven points, and the rest of the cards are their normal numeric value.

Winning Strategies

There are various strategies players should know when playing the game of rummy. The most important thing is observing your opponent's draws and discards. You'll want to memorize what cards your opponent is discarding and which discards he is taking into his hand. This lets you understand what cards are in your opponent's hand and also allows you to know what cards are unavailable to you for later play. If your opponent's discard doesn't create a meld in your hand, it might be better to draw from the stockpile. This is a better strategy for multiple reasons. It does not allow your opponent to read your hand, you are not picking up a card that is of no use to your opponent, and you might potentially destroy your opponent's hand with the card you pick up.

Knocking

In gin rummy, do not try to go for a gin hand. The bonus will not compensate for the times you lose when you should have knocked. A typical game ends somewhere between half and two-thirds of the deck, so if you can knock, do so by that point. If you are expecting a knock from your opponent, you will want to discard any cards of high value in your hand. If you knock, try to arrange your melds so that a card is attached to a three-of-a-kind (creating a four-of-a-kind) instead of a sequence, so that your opponent cannot continue the sequence.

Deadwoods

In the beginning of the game, you might want to hold any high-value deadwood cards in your hand so that your opponent may not use them. If you have a deadwood in your hand that is similar in value and suit to a discard from your opponent, go ahead and discard that card. There's a good chance that your opponent will not need that card.

Cards to Hold On To

Hold on to consecutive running cards. It doubles your chance of obtaining a sequence because you could get the high or low card of the run. (As an example, if you have the 5♠ 6♠, you can use either a 4♠ or 7♠ to create a sequence.) A seven of any suit is the most valuable card of the deck for its ability to extend melds. If you have a seven, try to keep it in your hand so it does not help your opponent as a discard.

Try holding back cards in your hand until later in the game. This prevents other players from using them and making more plays on the table. If you can play multiple melds, keep one in your hand. You can then lay it on the next hand and not have to pick up an extra card.

Chapter 13
Blackjack

Blackjack is the most popular gambling casino game of all, due to its simple rules and "beatability." By following the proper playing strategy, you can cut the house edge to almost zero or even gain the edge for yourself! This chapter introduces you to the basics of blackjack, so you'll be ready to play with a group of friends or at a table at the local casino.

History of the Game

Blackjack is said to have originated in France in the 1700s, where it was known by the name of *Vingt et Un* (Twenty-One). The game was introduced to the United States in the 1800s. In order to expose more players to the game, casinos offered to pay three-to-two odds if a player was dealt an ace of spades and a jack of spades as their first two cards. Players called that deal a blackjack (because black is the color of the spades) to differentiate it from a hand of twenty-one made with three or more cards. This was the origination of the name blackjack.

Blackjack became increasingly popular over the years, and by 1945 was only second in popularity to craps. By the late 1970s, it was recognized as the most popular gambling game. The first recognized effort to apply mathematics to blackjack began in 1953 and continues to this day. The first methods used calculators and statistical theory to determine the best methods of playing, but today multiple computers are used to simulate play.

The Object of the Game

Blackjack is an easy game to learn, but it's a difficult game to master. The rules are simple and straightforward, but there are various strategies in betting and playing the game. The objective of blackjack is to try to beat the dealer by getting closer than the dealer to twenty-one, without going over. If the total value of your cards is closer to twenty-one than the dealer's cards, or if the dealer goes over twenty-one, you win as much as you have bet. Blackjack (an ace and a ten or face card) typically pays 3:2, which means you win 1½ times your bet.

FACT

Most casinos use six or eight decks of cards when dealing out blackjack. There are two main reasons that they do this. One reason is to allow the dealer to deal more hands per hour and increase the casino take. It also reduces the player advantage gained from card counting.

A standard pack of fifty-two cards is used, although in some instances (especially in casinos) the game is played with multiple decks. The numbered cards are valued at their face value, and the face cards are valued at ten. An ace can be valued at either one or eleven, depending on which point value will benefit your hand. You can switch the value of an ace during the middle of the game if it is to your advantage. A hand containing an ace that is counted as an eleven is considered a "soft" hand—for instance, an ace and a five is a "soft sixteen"—because the hand could also have a value of six. A hand with no ace or with an ace counted as a one is called a "hard" hand; for example, a ten and a seven or an ace, six, and ten are both a "hard seventeen."

How to Play

After you place a bet in front of you on the table, the dealer deals one card face up to each player and one card face down to himself. This card is called the "hole card" because at one time it was placed in an indentation in the table. The dealer then deals a second card face up to each player and himself. If the dealer deals himself a ten or face card, he will then peek at the hole card to see if it is an ace. If the card is an ace, the dealer has blackjack and wins that hand automatically—end of game. In casinos, the dealer is also the banker and never changes. When you play at home, you can rotate the deal so that every player has a chance to be dealer.

In some Vegas casinos, players are dealt both cards face down. Almost everywhere else, the player's cards are dealt face up in an effort to prevent players from cheating. If the cards are dealt face up, do not touch them!

Playing Your Hand

After the deal, starting with the person to the dealer's left, each player has to decide what to do with his hand. If you are dealt a natural blackjack (a ten or court card and an ace), the dealer automatically pays you three to two on your bet. If you are not dealt a blackjack, you must make one or more moves. You can hit (take another card) if you want to try to get closer to twenty-one. In most casinos, you signal a hit by tapping the table with your index finger. If your cards were dealt face down, you may gesture by lightly flicking the cards across the table two times toward your body. If you bust, you lose, and the dealer immediately takes your original bet.

You can stand (take no more cards) at any time you are satisfied with the total of your cards. In most casinos, you signal a stand by waving your hand (palm down) from left to right about an inch over the table in a short gesture. If your cards were dealt face down, you may gesture by turning the cards in a horizontal direction or by placing the bet on top of the cards.

You also have the option to double down if you have been dealt two cards and believe that a third card will give you a total that will beat the dealer's hand. When you double down, you increase your bet (up to the amount of your original wager) but agree in exchange to take one, and only one, card. Typically, you would double down when your first two cards total eleven (or sometimes in cases when they total nine or ten). This allows you to take advantage of the chance that you may get a ten (very good, since there are many more ten-value cards than other numbers in the deck) on your next card, thus giving you twenty-one. However, once you get your third card, you must stand, even if you only get a two.

ALERT!

In some casinos, if you split two aces, you get only one additional card for each hand. If you split two aces and one or both of your hands totals twenty-one, this is not considered blackjack as far as payout is concerned, and you will be paid even money.

You may split your hand if you have two cards of the same value. This means that you will split them into two separate hands by betting the same amount as your original bet. You signify that you want to split by placing a second bet (of the same size) next to your first bet. Do not put your bet on top of your original bet, and do not touch the cards if they were dealt face up. The dealer will split your cards and then deal one card on top of your first split card. You can then choose to hit, stand, double down, or split again if the third card dealt gives you another pair. After you stand or bust on that hand, the dealer will deal a card onto your second split card. You have the same option as above, and your play is complete when you stand or bust your second hand.

If the casino permits it, you may surrender your cards by discarding the hand you were dealt and losing half of your bet. The only time you can do this is when you have your first two cards. This is a rarely accepted option and will be clearly noted on the table or before game play.

Taking Insurance

If the dealer has an ace as his face-up card, you have the choice of buying insurance against a dealer blackjack. This costs you half of your original bet. If the dealer does have blackjack, the insurance pays two to one, matching the amount of the player's original bet. If you choose to purchase insurance, and the dealer does not have blackjack, you lose your insurance bet. If both you and the dealer have blackjack, the game is considered a push.

Dealer Payout

After you have chosen to stand or you bust, the next player plays her hand. Play continues around the table until each player has completed his or her hand. The dealer then turns up his face-down card and fol-lows a strict set of rules based on the value of his hand. If the dealer has a value under seventeen, he must deal himself cards until his hand totals seventeen or above. If he busts, the dealer pays all players who have not busted. If the dealer does not bust, he compares the value of his hand to the value of each player who has not busted. If the dealer's total beats your total, he takes the bet. If his total is less than your total, you win the amount that you bet (called winning "even money"), including any additional bets in doubling down or splitting a pair. If the dealer's hand and your hand are equal, the hand is considered a "push" and you get back your original bet but don't win any additional money. A blackjack beats the dealer's count of twenty-one, which is why the dealer pays a blackjack before looking at his own cards.

When playing at home, you can add bonuses to dealer payouts. One bonus is that if you create twenty-one with five or more cards, you collect double your bet. If you create twenty-one with three sevens, you collect triple your bet. If you create twenty-one with a six, seven, and eight, you collect double your bet.

Basic Blackjack Strategy

Over the years, many experts have tried to develop strategies for winning the game of blackjack. The following strategy table was created through multiple computer simulations. In these simulations, the computer played tens of thousands of hands for each of the various situations and statistically determined what option of play most benefited the player. Under this system, your decisions in blackjack always depend on what the dealer is showing.

Strategies differ for games played using one deck and multiple decks. **TABLE 13-1** shows the strategy for a single deck of cards. The values across the top correspond to the dealer's up card. The player's hand is the values running down the left side of the table (farther down the table it shows soft hands and pairs). Where these two values intersect is the strategy for the player to play his hand. Insurance is never recommended. The strategy is very similar for multiple decks, but does vary in some hands. **TABLE 13-2** shows the strategy for multiple decks.

Many players follow this strategy. If you play an option not recommended in the table, you may find other players getting angry with you! Don't take it to heart, but do understand that if you play before another player, you can affect their hand by the way you play yours.

Table 13-1: Blackjack Strategy for One Deck

Your Hand	Dealer's Up Card									
	2	3	4	5	6	7	8	9	10	A
7 or less	H	H	H	H	H	H	H	H	H	H
8	H	H	H	D	D	H	H	H	H	H
9	D	D	D	D	D	H	H	H	H	H
10	D	D	D	D	D	D	D	D	H	H
11	D	D	D	D	D	D	D	D	D	D
12	H	H	S	S	S	H	H	H	H	H
13	S	S	S	S	S	H	H	H	H	H
14	S	S	S	S	S	H	H	H	H	H
15	S	S	S	S	S	H	H	H	H	H
16	S	S	S	S	S	H	H	H	H	H
17	S	S	S	S	S	S	S	S	S	S
A, 2	H	H	D	D	D	H	H	H	H	H
A, 3	H	H	D	D	D	H	H	H	H	H
A, 4	H	H	D	D	D	H	H	H	H	H
A, 5	H	H	D	D	D	H	H	H	H	H
A, 6	D	D	D	D	D	H	H	H	H	H
A, 7	S	D	D	D	D	S	S	H	H	S
A, 8	S	S	S	S	D	S	S	S	S	S
A, 9	S	S	S	S	S	S	S	S	S	S
A, A	P	P	P	P	P	P	P	P	P	P
2, 2	H	P	P	P	P	P	H	H	H	H
3, 3	H	H	P	P	P	P	H	H	H	H
4, 4	H	H	H	D	D	H	H	H	H	H
5, 5	D	D	D	D	D	D	D	D	H	H
6, 6	P	P	P	P	P	H	H	H	H	H
7, 7	P	P	P	P	P	P	H	H	S	H
8, 8	P	P	P	P	P	P	P	P	P	P
9, 9	P	P	P	P	P	S	P	P	S	S
10, 10	S	S	S	S	S	S	S	S	S	S

H=HIT, S=STAND, D=DOUBLE DOWN, P=SPLIT PAIR

Table 13-2: Blackjack Strategy for Multiple Decks

Your Hand	Dealer's Up Card									
	2	3	4	5	6	7	8	9	10	A
7 or less	H	H	H	H	H	H	H	H	H	H
8	H	H	H	H	H	H	H	H	H	H
9	H	D	D	D	D	H	H	H	H	H
10	D	D	D	D	D	D	D	D	H	H
11	D	D	D	D	D	D	D	D	D	H
12	H	H	S	S	S	H	H	H	H	H
13	S	S	S	S	S	H	H	H	H	H
14	S	S	S	S	S	H	H	H	H	H
15	S	S	S	S	S	H	H	H	H	H
16	S	S	S	S	S	H	H	H	H	H
17	S	S	S	S	S	S	S	S	S	S
A, 2	H	H	H	D	D	H	H	H	H	H
A, 3	H	H	H	D	D	H	H	H	H	H
A, 4	H	H	D	D	D	H	H	H	H	H
A, 5	H	H	D	D	D	H	H	H	H	H
A, 6	H	H	D	D	D	H	H	H	H	H
A, 7	S	D	D	D	D	S	S	H	H	S
A, 8	S	S	S	S	S	S	S	S	S	S
A, 9	S	S	S	S	S	S	S	S	S	S
A, A	P	P	P	P	P	P	P	P	P	P
2, 2	P	P	P	P	P	P	H	H	H	H
3, 3	P	P	P	P	P	P	H	H	H	H
4, 4	H	H	H	D	D	H	H	H	H	H
5, 5	D	D	D	D	D	D	D	D	H	H
6, 6	P	P	P	P	P	H	H	H	H	H
7, 7	P	P	P	P	P	P	H	H	H	H
8, 8	P	P	P	P	P	P	P	P	P	P
9, 9	P	P	P	P	P	S	P	P	S	S
10, 10	S	S	S	S	S	S	S	S	S	S

H=HIT, S=STAND, D=DOUBLE DOWN, P=SPLIT PAIR

Counting Cards

Another strategy that blackjack players use to help them on their road to victory (and hopefully a lot of money!) is counting cards. Having an idea of what cards are still left to come can help you make smarter bets. When there are many more high cards in the deck than low cards, there are more chances that the dealer will bust, since he is required to hit if his cards total less than seventeen. Likewise, if there are more low cards left in the deck than high cards, the dealer has a better chance of beating you. So if you can determine at least roughly what cards remain in the deck, you'll know whether you should be betting more money or keeping your bets small.

When playing with one or two decks, you may find it easy to memorize the cards that have been played, furthering your chances of winning as the deck(s) are depleted, because you know what cards are left. With multiple decks and in casinos, there are variations on counting cards that help a player to maximize his earnings.

Casual Card Counting

Casual card counting is a method that requires no mathematics and hardly any concentration. The object is just to observe the flow of cards coming from the deck. If you notice that a good number of face cards and aces have been played recently, it's time to rein in your bet. If a lot of low cards have been played, it's a good time to up your bet. Look for obvious extremes. If the cards are flowing out relatively evenly, you'll want to employ some of the betting strategies listed later.

High-Low Card Counting

The high-low system of counting cards is a popular method for keeping track of what is going on with the decks. In this system, you apply a value of –1 to any high cards (aces, face cards, or tens). A value of +1 is applied to low cards (two, three, four, five, or six). A value of 0 is assigned to any middle cards (seven, eight, or nine). As each hand is dealt, keep a running tally of points, and make your wagering decisions based on what the total is. When the total is positive, the advantage is yours, and you should increase your wager. When the total is negative, the advantage is to the dealer and you should decrease your wager. As the game progresses through the decks, the accuracy of the running tally becomes greater, and the wagers can be increased or decreased accordingly.

Betting Strategies

Betting strategies are used in blackjack to help the player walk away with some money left in her pocket, or, even better yet, as a winner! You can choose to use the progressive betting method, where your bet will increase progressively as you win. Another option is the Martingale method, where you increase your bet as you lose.

Progressive Betting with Two Levels

This betting strategy is simple and can be very effective. You must first establish a low bet and a high bet that you will carry throughout your blackjack game. If you win a hand, you bet the high amount on the next hand. If you lose a hand, you bet the low amount on the next hand. If you win once and continue to win, you continue to bet the high amount until you lose again. As an example, let's say you choose a low bet of $10 and a high bet of $25. If you win your first hand, you bet $25 for the next hand. If you lose that hand, you bet $10 for the next hand. You continue to bet $10 a hand until you win, and then bet $25 for that next hand. The theory here is that when you get on a winning streak you will win much more than you will lose on a losing streak.

Progressive Betting with Five Levels

This betting strategy is slightly more complex. You first establish a low bet. You then follow a 1-2-3-5-1 progression for successive hands, in which if you continue to win you start by betting your original bet, then two times that amount, three times, five times, and then back down to your original bet. As an example, let's say you choose a low bet of $5. If you win the first hand, you bet $10 on the second hand. If you win the second hand, you bet $15 on the third hand. If you win the third hand, you bet $25 on the fourth hand. If you win that hand, you drop back down to a $5 bet. If at any point during the progression you lose a hand, you drop your bet back down to $5 until you win a hand again.

In a standard deck of fifty-two cards, there are sixteen cards with a value of ten—four tens, four jacks, four queens, and four kings. This group represents 30.8 percent of a deck and gives you high odds of having at least one card worth ten in each hand.

The assumption of this strategy is that you will have winning streaks and losing streaks as you play. The goal of the progressive betting is that as you win, you continue to bet more and win more, but when you hit the losing streak you bet even and don't lose nearly as much as you've won.

Martingale System

This betting strategy has you doubling your bet every time you lose a hand. When you finally win a hand, your bet returns to your minimum and you recover your losses with one win. As an example, you bet $2 in one hand and lose. You bet $4 in the next hand and lose, $8 in the next hand and lose, $16 in the next hand and win that hand. You now have a profit of $2. Realizing a profit with the one winning hand only works if you are not doubling down or splitting in various hands. In those cases, if you lost both hands, you would not have a profit when you finally win. The biggest problem with this particular system is that you may quickly run out of money if you hit a very long losing streak! Or you may very well hit the maximum table bet and not be able to recover all your losses with one bet.

Chapter 14
Poker Basics

Poker is the most popular gambling card game and is played everywhere card games are played. There are literally hundreds of versions of poker available to play, and you can play it at home, in a casino, or on the Internet. You can play poker for pennies or for thousands of dollars. Regardless, every poker player plays with a little luck and a lot of tactics that you'll learn here.

History of the Game

Poker, its name, and its history are a great mystery to those who study and play the game. There are no specific ancestors of poker to derive a date from, but because of its basic principle, it is considered very old. The earliest knowledge of the game in the United States comes from a reference to the game being played in 1834 on Mississippi riverboats. Poker appeared to be more legitimate than three-card monte, and so it attracted quite a following of "honest" gamblers. Modifications to the game, such as stud poker, draw, and the straight, became popular during the Civil War, and the joker was introduced as a wild card in 1875.

QUESTION?

Do I play poker with money?
Poker is traditionally played with chips (plastic disks of various colors) that designate monetary amounts. Choose one player to be the banker, and she will keep track of the different value of the chips and who has paid in what dollar amount.

There are various theories about the origin of the name of poker. Some claim it is a derivative of the French game Poque. Others state that is from the German game Pochspiel, which has an element of bluffing, or Hindu's Pukka. Another theory is that poker is a variation of the slang "poke," a term used by pickpockets. Poker has continued to evolve over the years and has a colorful past in saloons, game halls, and casinos. Whatever its origin, poker has become the most popular card game and even boasts many tournaments and competitions.

Elements of Poker

You have to know the basics of poker before sitting down to play a game. There are specific rankings of poker hands, odds for betting, odds for bettering your hand, rules for betting, and more. Poker is a game in which everyone plays for himself. There are no teams or partnerships, and you want to win as much money as you can through betting and playing your hands wisely. You can play poker with anywhere from two to thirteen players, but you'll find that it's usually best played with five to eight players. Poker is played with a standard deck of fifty-two cards, although some games require more decks and cards added, such as adding jokers as wild cards. The cards rank from high to low as ace, king, queen, jack, ten, nine, eight, seven, six, five, four, three, and two.

Poker Hands

There are four suits: hearts, diamonds, clubs, and spades. No suit is higher than the other. A poker hand is made with five cards. The hands rank from high to low as follows:

- **Five of a kind:** This hand only exists if you are playing with wild cards (for instance, joker A♥ A♠ A♦ A♣).
- **Royal flush:** The sequence of cards, 10 J Q K A, all in the same suit.
- **Straight flush:** Any sequence of cards, all in the same suit (such as 5♥ 6♥ 7♥ 8♥ 9♥). If there is a tie, the player with the higher straight wins.
- **Four of a kind:** Four cards of the same value (such as 8♥ 8♠ 8♦ 8♣), and one card of a different value.
- **Full house:** Three cards of one value and a pair (such as 2♥ 2♠ 2♣ 6♦ 6♥). When there is a tie, the higher three-of-a-kind wins the hand. If they are the same value, the higher pair wins.
- **Flush:** Any five cards of the same suit (such as A♣ 4♣ 5♣ 9♣ K♣). When there is a tie, the flush with the highest card wins. If they are the same value, the second highest card wins, and so on.
- **Straight:** Any five consecutive cards in any combination of suits (such as 9♦ 10♦ J♣ Q♥ K♣). When there are two straights, the higher straight wins.
- **Three of a kind:** Three cards of the same value and two cards of differing values. When there is a tie, the higher three-of-a-kind wins. If they are the same value, the highest of the other cards (called kickers) wins.
- **Two pair:** Two sets of two cards of the same value (such as 4♦ 4♣ Q♥ Q♦) and one card of a differing value. When there is a tie, the highest pair wins the hand. If the high pairs are the same value, the higher second pair wins.

- **Pair:** Two cards of the same value and three cards of differing values. When there are two pairs, the higher pair wins the hand. If they are the same value, the highest kicker wins.
- **High card:** The highest card in a mix of five dissimilar cards. When there is a tie, the second highest card wins.

Odds

Experts play the game of poker with a good understanding of the odds. Knowing what the odds are of being dealt a specific hand in poker doesn't do much to improve your game. But knowing the difference between "pot odds" and "card odds" can help you formulate your betting strategy and, in the long run, help make you a winning player. Card odds describe the probability that you'll improve your hand with a draw or the next round of dealing. To gauge your card odds, consider how many cards are left in the deck that can improve your hand. For example, if you hold four cards to a flush, you need one more card of that suit to make the flush. There are thirteen cards in each suit (if you're playing without wild cards), and you hold four of them, so there are nine more cards that can help your hand. You've only seen five of the fifty-two cards in the deck (those in your hand), but you know that there are thirty-eight cards that will *not* help your hand (52 – 5 – 9 = 38). Therefore, the odds of drawing a flush with the next card are nine in thirty-eight (or slightly more than one in four). In a game where you can see some of the cards held by your opponents, you must take these into consideration too. If an opponent is showing a card of your suit, that's one less card available to make your flush.

Pot odds are easy to figure. This is the ratio of the amount of money you have to put in to the value of the pot. If the pot is worth $100 and you have to put in $5 to continue playing, the pot odds are 20 to 1, so if you hold a hand that has better than 1:20 odds of improving to a winning hand, you should call a bet.

In the above example of a four-card flush, your chances are 1:4 of making the flush. You should therefore call a bet only if the pot odds are better than 4:1. In the case of a $5 bet, you should call a bet if the pot size is greater than $20.

Betting

In most versions of poker, you ante for the right to play before the cards are dealt. Some games call for a "forced bring-in," in which a player is required to bet to start the action; in seven-card stud, the player with the lowest up-card has to make the forced bring-in to get things started. Other games, like Texas Hold 'Em and Omaha, have blind bets ("blinds"), which are similar to the bring-in; blinds are paid by the player or players to the left of the dealer's button.

FACT

The term "bad beat" in poker is when you have a good hand, but a better hand beats it. In some instances your hand was the favorite to win in the beginning of the hand but ends up losing at the end. In some cases you may have a very high hand, but another player has an even higher hand!

After the antes, bring-ins, and blinds, betting rules vary according to the version of poker you're playing. You have four choices when it is your turn to bet:

- **Check:** You pass the betting on to the next player if there are no bets already on the table. You are in essence making a zero bet.
- **Call:** You stay in the hand by adding enough money to the pot to cover all of the previous bets made by players who acted before you. For example, if your opponent bets $5, you would need to call $5 to remain in the hand.
- **Raise:** You raise by calling the previous bets and adding an additional amount into the pot. In the previous example, you could raise your opponent by putting in $10 (calling his $5 bet and raising another $5).
- **Fold:** You fold by discarding your cards and dropping out of the hand. You lose any money that you have already placed in the pot.

Betting usually proceeds clockwise around the table until each player has either called all bets or folded. Some poker games have specified numbers of betting rounds interspersed with the receipt or replacement of cards.

Five-Card Draw Poker

Five-card draw poker is one of two original games of poker. In a draw poker game, you discard cards in your hand and draw new ones in the hopes of building a better hand to win the pot. You'll need at least one other player and a deck of fifty-two cards. You and your opponents start out a game of five-card draw by anteing into the pot.

The First Round of Betting

A random dealer is selected and deals clockwise five cards, face down, one at a time to each player. The deal will continue to rotate in a clockwise direction after each hand is played.

The players pick up their cards and assess their hands. The player to the left of the dealer opens the betting round by betting, checking, or folding his hand. Play goes around the table until each player has called all bets or folded his cards. In the Jackpot version of draw poker, you must have a pair of jacks or better to open the betting. If nobody can open, the hands are thrown in and re-dealt. In Progressive Jackpot, if a hand is thrown in because nobody had a pair of jacks, you must have a pair of queens or better to open the betting in the next hand. If that hand is thrown in as well, you must have a pair of kings or better to open the betting in the third hand and a pair of aces or better to open betting in the fourth hand.

Discarding/Replacing

You now have the choice of discarding any cards in your hand, which will be replaced by the dealer from the deck. You do this in the hopes of creating a better hand with any of the cards you choose to keep. The player to the dealer's left starts by laying any discarded cards, face down, on the table. The dealer then replaces those cards, face down, with enough cards to bring your hand back up to five. This continues around the table until each player has drawn any cards he wishes, and another round of betting occurs.

Winning/Showdown

If at any time during the two betting rounds, there is only one person remaining (that is, if every other player folds), that player wins and takes the pot. If there are two or more players remaining after the final betting round, the players have reached the showdown and they must reveal their hands. The player with the best poker hand wins and takes the pot.

Five-Card Stud Poker

Five-card stud is the other standard poker game. Five-card stud is the original stud game and was very popular until seven-card stud came along. Because this game does not have a discard-and-replace option, the winning hands are typically low in value. To play five-card stud, you need a deck of fifty-two cards and at least two players. The maximum number of players is ten unless you add another deck of cards. You should agree upon a minimum bet before starting the game.

Setting Up the Hands

Five-card stud opens with a random dealer being chosen. Each player antes, and the dealer deals clockwise one card face down to each player. He then deals another card face up (the "door" card) to each player. Deal will continue to rotate in a clockwise direction after each hand is played.

FACT

Poker games are defined by their betting limits. Betting limits usually are either "spread limit" or "structured limit." Spread limits are expressed as a range, such as $1–$5. This means that the minimum bet is $1, the maximum bet is $5, and players are free to bet or raise anything in between. In structured-limit games (such as $2/$4), bets and raises in early rounds are always at the lower limit and at the higher limit in later rounds; players decide whether to bet or raise, but the amount of the bet or raise is determined by the limit.

The player with the highest door card opens the betting. If there is a tie for the high card, the player closest to the dealer's left becomes the first bettor. The player with the highest door card must "bring it in" by betting an amount at least equal to the minimum bet. If you don't want to bet, you can fold your hand, and play moves clockwise. Once a player bets, the remaining players must either fold, call the bet, or raise the bet.

The Streets

After the round of betting is complete, the dealer deals a third card face up to each player—thus beginning "third street" because everyone has three cards. In this round of betting, and in following rounds, the player who holds the best hand in his open cards begins the betting. Following this second round of betting, fourth street and fifth street are played, with the dealer dealing another card face up, followed by rounds of betting.

It is the dealer's responsibility, after dealing out each round of cards, to dictate the first bettor by looking at the open cards of each player and determining the best hand. He does this by saying "Pair of fives bets" or "Three-of-a-kind bets." During fourth and fifth street, the dealer should also indicate any hands that might become straights or flushes. A potential straight or flush does not become the best hand showing to start the betting, but it does help you determine if you want to stay in the game or fold.

Winning/Showdown

If at any time during the betting rounds there is only one person remaining (that is, every other player folds), that player wins and takes the pot. You are not required to show your hand if everybody folds to you. If there are two or more players remaining at the end of fifth street, the players have reached the showdown and they must reveal their hands. The player with the best hand wins and takes the pot.

Seven-Card Stud Poker

Seven-card stud is a very popular and demanding poker game that incorporates different betting and playing techniques depending on what street the current deal is on. You need two to eight players and a standard deck of fifty-two cards to play. You all need to agree on a minimum bet, and that becomes the ante that you each contribute to the pot before starting play.

Setting Up the Hands

Seven-card stud opens with a random dealer being chosen. Clockwise, he deals two cards, one at a time, face down to each player. He then deals the door card face-up to each player. At this time, the game is at third street because each player has three cards in his hand. Deal will continue to rotate in a clockwise direction after each hand is played.

ALERT!

Even though each player is dealt seven cards in seven-card stud, the winning hand is made from only the best five cards for that hand. Do not make the mistake of thinking that you are going to win with three pairs!

The player with the highest door card opens the betting. If there is a tie for the high card, the player closest to the dealer's left becomes the first bettor. The player with the highest door card must bet an amount at least equal to the minimum bet. If he doesn't want to bet, he can fold his hand, and play moves clockwise. Once a player bets, the remaining players must either fold, call the bet, or raise the bet.

The Streets

After the first round of betting is complete, the dealer deals one card face up to each player—thus beginning fourth street. In this hand, and in following hands, the first player to begin the round of betting is the player with the best hand in his open cards. During fifth and sixth street, the dealer continues to deal one card face up with a round of betting in between. During seventh street, the dealer deals one card face down.

Winning/Showdown

If at any time during the betting rounds, there is only one person remaining (that is, every other player folds), that player wins and takes the pot. If there are two or more players remaining, the players have reached the showdown. You must pick up your cards and build your best five-card poker hand. You discard two cards face down and reveal your five cards to your opponents. The player with the best hand wins and takes the pot.

Chapter 15
Variations on Poker

Although the basics of poker always remain the same, there are many variations that have been introduced to the game. This chapter introduces you to some of the more popular variations of poker, such as Texas Hold 'Em and Omaha. You'll also learn a couple of silly and simple adaptations to the game with Guts and Indian Poker.

Texas Hold 'Em

You don't have to live in Texas to play Texas Hold 'Em. This game has recently become very popular in casinos that have poker table rooms. It's a difficult game to master but an easy game to learn. With just a few practice lessons you will be able to play on the table, but you'll need to play multiple hands to learn when to bet and when to fold. You'll need at least two players and a standard deck of fifty-two cards to start playing this game.

Dealing the Hand

Texas Hold 'Em opens with the two players to the left of the dealer placing out a predetermined amount of money (the blinds) so there is an initial pot to play for. The first player to the left of the dealer posts the small blind, and it is typically equal to half of the minimum bid declared at the table. The second player posts the big blind, and it is equal to the minimum bid declared. The dealer deals clockwise, two face-down cards, one at a time to each player. Deal will continue to rotate in a clockwise direction after each hand is played. If you're playing at a casino, deal will not rotate, but there will be a marker to indicate whose turn it is to post the blinds.

QUESTION?

Why doesn't every player have to ante?
Although it appears that the players posting the blinds are getting the short end of the stick, that isn't actually the case. Since deal rotates to the left, eventually every player will either have to post a small blind and a big blind or leave the table before their turn.

Multiple Rounds of Betting

The game begins with everyone picking up their cards and assessing their hands. The player to the left of the two who posted the blinds opens the first betting round by calling the bet, raising, or folding his hand. Play continues clockwise around the table with each player calling, raising, or folding his hand until all bets are equal.

After the betting round is over, the dealer burns (or discards) a card from the stockpile and then flips the next three cards, known as the flop, face up on the table. These cards are community cards shared by every player at the table. These cards make a five-card hand, combined with the two cards you hold.

Another round of betting starts with the player to the dealer's left. In this round and in future rounds of betting, a player can check, bet, raise, or fold his hand. After everyone has called the bets or folded, the dealer burns another card from the stockpile and flips over the next card (known as the turn) onto the table. Now you can use the four communal cards with the two cards that you hold to make the best five-card poker hand.

Another round of betting starts with the player to the dealer's left. After the betting is complete, the dealer burns another card and flips over the next (and last) card (called the river) onto the table. You can now use any combination of the five cards on the table and the two cards you hold to form the best possible five-card poker hand. One final round of betting occurs.

FACT

If you've ever watched the World Series of Poker on the Travel Channel, you've seen Texas Hold 'Em, widely considered the game of choice among professional poker players. The version most popularly played in tournaments is played with no betting limits— players can bet any amount at any time.

Winning/Showdown

If at any time during the betting rounds there is only one person remaining (that is, every other player folds), that player wins and takes the pot. If there are two or more players remaining, you have reached the showdown and must reveal your hands. The player with the best hand wins and takes the pot. If any two hands tie, the players split the pot and each wins half.

Omaha

Omaha resembles Texas Hold 'Em in that it uses five communal cards, but players get four "hole" cards that only they see. In Omaha, players *must* use two and only two of the cards in their hand plus three of the communal cards to make their hand. You'll need at least two players and a standard deck of fifty-two cards to play Omaha.

Dealing the Hand

A random dealer is selected, and the two players to the left of the dealer post the big and small blinds. The dealer then deals four hole cards clockwise, face down, one at a time to each player. Deal will continue to rotate in a clockwise direction after each hand is played. If you're playing at a casino, deal will not rotate, but there will be a marker to indicate whose turn it is to post the blinds.

Rounds of Betting

The game begins with all players picking up their cards and assessing their hands. The player to the left of the two who posted the blinds opens the betting round by calling the bet, raising, or folding his hand. Play continues clockwise around the table until everyone has called the bets or folded.

After the round is over, the dealer burns the top card by placing it at the bottom of the deck or in the middle of the deck and then flips the next three cards up on the table. This is called the flop. These cards can be used by any of the players to make a five-card poker hand with two of the four cards they hold. You don't pick these cards up because they are communal to everyone.

Another round of betting starts with the player to the dealer's left. If that player has folded his hand, the betting starts with the first person who is still in the game. In this round and in future rounds of betting, a player can check, bet, raise, or fold his hand. After all bets have been played and called, the dealer burns another card and flips over the next card (known as the turn) onto the table.

Another round of betting begins with the first player still in the game to the dealer's left. When it is over, the dealer burns another card and flips over the next (and last) card (called the river) onto the table. You must now use two of the cards in your hand and any three of the cards on the table to form your best five-card hand. One final round of betting occurs.

FACT

Omaha High-Low (also called Omaha Eight or Better) is a split-pot game where the player with the highest hand wins half of the pot, and the winner of the lowest hand wins the other half. It can be a very exciting game—there will be players raising the bets to win with a high hand and players raising the bets to win with a low hand, and you never know who is who!

Winning/Showdown

If at any time during the betting rounds, there is only one person remaining (that is, every other player folds), that player wins and takes the pot. If there are two or more players remaining, you have reached the showdown and must reveal your hands. The player with the best hand wins and takes the pot. If any two hands tie, the players split the pot.

Caribbean Poker

Caribbean Poker is a variation of poker that is not the typical betting game. You each play your hand individually against the dealer or bank instead of against other players. You'll need at least two players and a standard pack of fifty-two cards to start up a game of Caribbean Poker. After each player antes, you are dealt five cards and the bank is dealt five cards. Your cards are all dealt face down. The bank is dealt four cards face down and one card face up.

You each pick up your cards and determine if you want to surrender against the bank's up card or to continue playing by making a call bet and doubling your original ante. If you are still in the game, you and the bank turn over your hands in a showdown. If the bank does not have at least an ace-king high (or better), your bet is automatically returned and the bank pays out an amount equal to the original ante. If the bank does have a qualifying hand, the bank compares his hand to each player's. If your hand loses to the bank's hand, you lose your ante and call bet. If your hand beats the bank's hand, the bank will pay out even money for the ante and fixed odds on your call bet, as follows:

- Even odds **(1:1)** for a pair or high card
- **2:1** odds for two pairs
- **3:1** odds for three of a kind
- **4:1** odds for a straight
- **5:1** odds for a flush
- **20:1** odds for a four of a kind
- **50:1** odds for a straight flush
- **100:1** odds for a royal flush

When you and the bank have equal hands it is considered a "push," and all money bet is returned without further payout.

Chinese Poker

Chinese Poker is a great variation of poker that is different than the typical stud and draw games. It is meant for smaller groups of people with just two to four players, and players bet with points instead of chips. Each point is worth a specific dollar amount, so it's still a gambling game and you can still win or lose large amounts of money. Chinese Poker opens with a dealer being chosen at random and dealing out thirteen cards, face down, to each player.

You begin by picking up your cards and arranging them into three distinct hands—the back hand, middle hand, and front hand. The front hand has three cards and must be lower in value than the middle hand. The middle hand has five cards and must be lower in value than the back hand, which also contains five cards. Straights and flushes do not count in the front hand. You then arrange your three hands in front of you (face down) with the back hand closest to you, the middle hand in the middle, and the front hand farthest away.

When you have all chosen your hands and laid out your cards, you turn over your hands and compare them against each of the other players' hands, one at a time. If there are four players, you will make three comparisons, one with each of the opponents. There are various ways to score the hand, and players should agree on the scoring system before play.

- **2–4 scoring:** The player with the higher back hand gets one point, the player with the higher middle hand gets one point, and the player with the higher front hand gets one point. Any bonus points (explained below) are added to the player's total. The player with the higher total gets an additional point (overall point). The player with the higher total gets the difference in points between the two scores.
- **1–4 scoring:** This scoring system is the same as the 2–4 scoring, except no overall point is added.
- **1–6 scoring:** If a player wins two out of three hands against another player, she scores one point. If she outranks all three hands, she scores six points.

Players also have the option to surrender their hands if they feel they have really bad cards and pay a set amount to each opponent before turning over their cards and comparing it to their opponents' hands. Whether to include this option, and the amount to pay, should be determined before play begins.

Bonuses are also given for high-ranking hands. A straight flush receives four bonus points, a four-of-a-kind receives three bonus points, a three-of-a-kind in the front hand receives two bonus points, and a full house in the middle hand receives one bonus point.

The Game of Guts

Guts is a poker game played with only three cards, so up to seventeen players can play with a standard deck of fifty-two cards. The name derives from a player needing enough "guts" to stay in the game. Each player chooses to be "in" or "out"—if you're out, you sit out the rest of the hand. If you stay in, your hand is compared with all other hands that stayed in. The best hand collects the pot, and the losers must match the value of the pot.

Guts opens with a random dealer being chosen. Players each ante, and then the dealer deals clockwise three cards, one at a time, face down to each player. Deal will continue to rotate in a clockwise direction after each hand is played.

After the deal, you pick up your cards and assess your hand. All players must declare simultaneously whether they are in or out. This can be done in one of several ways. You can hold your hand over the table and at the dealer's cue, drop the cards if you do not want to play. Or you can place a poker chip in your hand if you intend to drop your cards, and at the dealer's cue, you all open your hands to reveal your decision.

ALERT!

The ranking of hands in Guts is obviously different than standard five-card poker because it contains only three cards. From high to low, the hands rank as follows: straight flush, three-of-a-kind, straight, flush, pair, and high card.

If all players drop, a new hand is dealt. In the "wimp" variation of Guts, if all players drop, the player who had the highest hand has to match the pot instead of each player re-anteing. If only one player remains after the players drop, he wins the pot. If there are two or more players remaining, you have reached the showdown and must reveal your hands. The player with the best hand wins and takes the pot, and the other players who were still in the game must pay into the pot an equal amount of what was in it. This money starts the pot for the next hand and the players do not ante.

Mexican Stud

Mexican Stud is similar to the stud poker games, with a "roll your own" variation in which you decide what cards to show your opponents. This makes for a much more exciting and strategic game, because you never know if your opponents are showing their weak cards or their best cards. The first step is to choose a dealer at random. Players ante, and the dealer deals clockwise two hole cards, one at a time, face down to each player. Deal will continue to rotate in a clockwise direction after each hand is played.

After the deal is complete, players turn up a card of their choice, and the player to the left of the dealer starts a round of betting—he checks, bets, or folds his hand. The next players follow and can fold, call, or raise that bet.

After the round of betting is complete, the dealer deals one card face down to each player. As before, you view your hole cards and determine which one of these two cards to turn up. Another round of betting occurs, and this process continues until each player has four cards face up and one card face down.

If at any time during the betting rounds there is only one person remaining (that is, every other player folds), that player wins and takes the pot. If two or more players remain, those players must reveal their hands. The player with the best hand wins and takes the pot.

Pai Gow Poker

The traditional Asian game of Pai Gow is played with tiles that resemble dominos. An American version was introduced using standard playing cards and the ranking of hands was fashioned after poker hands, creating Pai Gow Poker. Like Caribbean Poker, Pai Gow Poker is a one-on-one game, played against the dealer instead of against other players. The object is to use seven cards to create two poker hands that will beat the dealer's hands.

Pai Gow Poker begins with each player placing a bet on the table. The dealer then shuffles the cards and deals out seven stacks with seven cards each, no matter how many players there are. The dealer rolls three dice and counts the total around the table counter-clockwise, starting with himself, to determine who gets the first hand. The remaining players get their hands in a counterclockwise rotation.

Ranking of Hands

The ranking of the cards in Pai Gow Poker is the same as poker—ace, king, queen, jack, ten, nine, eight, seven, six, five, four, three, and two. The suits are all equal in value. There is an exception in the ranking of hands in Pai Gow Poker, as follows:

- The highest straight is A K Q J 10.
- The second-highest straight is A 2 3 4 5.
- The third-highest straight is K Q J 10 9.

Pai Gow Poker is played with a joker as a wild card, but this card can only be used as an ace or to complete a royal flush, straight flush, flush, or straight.

Playing

You start the game by picking up your cards and building two hands, one with five cards and one with two cards. You then lay down your cards face up, the two-card hand on top and the five-card hand on the bottom.

FACT

In Pai Gow Poker, your five-card hand must have a higher value than your two-card hand. If your two-card hand is higher, it is a "foul" and you automatically lose. As an example, if you are dealt only one pair and can form no higher hands (flushes, straights)— the pair must be in your hand of five cards.

The dealer turns over his hands and compares them to each player's hands in turn. If the dealer loses to both of your hands, you win an amount equal to your initial bet minus a 5-percent commission. If the dealer's hands outrank both of your hands, you lose your bet. If the dealer wins a hand and you win a hand, it is a push and nobody wins or loses. If your hand ties (or copies) the dealer, the dealer wins.

Pyramid Poker

Pyramid Poker is a poker variation that also uses communal cards to help players build their hands. The cards are dealt in the shape of a pyramid, thus naming the game. You'll need at least two players and a standard deck of fifty-two cards. The first step is to choose a random dealer. Each player antes, and the dealer deals clockwise four cards face down to each player. He then deals six cards, face down, in the shape of a pyramid (one on the top row, two in the middle row, three on the bottom row). Deal will continue to rotate in a clockwise direction after each hand is played.

The game begins with a round of betting starting to the dealer's left. Each player can check (if no bets have been placed) or bet, call, raise, or fold in turn. The dealer then turns over the middle row and the middle card in the bottom row of the pyramid. A second round of betting takes place, after which the dealer turns over the top card. A third round of betting occurs. The dealer turns over the last two cards, and a final round of betting takes place.

You can use the four cards in your hand and any three cards that form an outside row of the pyramid to form your best five-card poker hand. Another variation of Pyramid Poker lets you use the four cards in your hand plus one card from each of three rows to form the best five-card poker hand. The player with the highest hand wins and takes the pot.

Chapter 16

Games with Wild Cards

Just one wild card can be the ticket to turning a promising hand into a winning hand! With a wild card, you can turn a mess of cards into a straight, a flush, or add to your pair or three-of-a-kind. Wild cards were introduced to games with the addition of the joker card, but they have since expanded to include various suited cards within the deck. Many games use wild cards, so have fun and go wild!

The Game of Fifty-Two

Fifty-Two is a fun and fast-paced spin on the traditional game of five-card draw. The game includes a ton of wild cards and it doesn't end like typical draw games. Instead, it continues hand after hand until all but one player drops out of the game. If you're that last player, you win and can win big! You'll need a deck of cards and at least one other player to play the game. It's best played with a large group of people.

A Round of Betting

Fifty-Two begins with the dealer naming three different values of the deck as wild cards, such as fives, nines, and queens. All players ante and place one coin on the table in front of them. This coin is used to indicate whether you plan to continue playing each hand. The dealer then deals five cards face down to each player.

With the many different combinations of wild cards, it's a good idea to jot down your combination when you deal. Classic wild card combinations include: fives, nines, and queens; twos, threes, and fours; aces, kings, and eights; threes, fives, and sevens; twos, fours, and tens; threes, sevens, and jacks; fives, sevens, and nines; and fours, sixes, and eights.

You evaluate your cards, and then there is a round of betting. (Because of the high number of wild cards, it is common for many or all of the players to stay in on the initial round of betting.) You secretly decide whether or not you'll stay in the game by first shielding the coin with your cards. If you wish to continue playing, you turn the coin heads-up. If you want to fold your hand, you turn your coin heads-down. You continue to shield your decision from the rest of the table. Once each player has set his cards down, it's time to reveal whether you'll remain in the game. The player to the dealer's left starts by revealing his coin, and this continues one at a time around the table.

Winning the Game

Players who remain in the game can choose to discard up to three cards from their hand, to be replaced by the dealer. Once the dealer has replaced any discarded cards, the players who remain reveal their hands, with the highest poker hand winning the pot. If two players each have the same high hand, the player who used the fewest wild cards in his hand wins.

But Fifty-Two doesn't end there. If you remained in the game but lost with a lesser hand, you must pay the pot an amount equal to the money that was won by the player who won the hand! This could multiply the pot by quite a bit if multiple players stayed in the round. Players who dropped out during the first round now return for another hand, and now there is no ante because the pot already has money in it. The deal is passed, and the new dealer reshuffles and deals, but the original wild cards declared at the opening of the game remain the same. Another hand is played, only now more money is at stake since the pot keeps growing. You will again use the coin on the table to show whether you plan to play or fold that round, and if you stay in and lose, you'll have to match the pot again. Play continues around the table, and the pot grows until only one player turns his coin heads-up during the betting round. At this stage, players usually don't want to continue playing if they have bad hands because they risk losing a great deal of money if they have to match the pot again. The one player who turned his coin heads-up wins the final round and—potentially—a ton of money!

ESSENTIAL

Don't forget that you're never out of the game for good until one person remains. So if you're dealt a card with low numbers and no wilds, don't turn up your coin in the hopes of getting three good cards on the discard. Wait for the next hand to play.

If only one player turns his coin heads-up during the opening round, he automatically takes the pot. If everyone goes tails-up during any round, you each pay the price of the original ante into the pot, and cards are shuffled and re-dealt by the next dealer.

Criss-Cross

Criss-Cross is a poker variation that uses five communal cards built out in the shape of a cross. Players choose three of those cards to help their hands (either the row or the column). The middle card of the cross is wild. You'll need to grab up to ten players and a standard deck of fifty-two cards.

Criss-Cross opens with a random dealer being chosen. Once all antes are in, the dealer deals clockwise four cards, one at a time, face down to each player. He then deals five communal cards face down on the table in a cross pattern, so that three cards are in a row and three cards are in a column. A sample deal (with the cards turned up) looks like this:

Q♥

4♣ 3♠ J♠

8♥

Betting

The dealer turns over one of the outside communal cards, and a round of betting begins. The player to the left of the dealer opens the round. Each player can check (if there are no bets before him), bet, call, raise, or fold. After the round is over, the dealer flips over another outside card, and another round of betting occurs. This continues until the dealer has flipped over the middle card as the last card. This card becomes a wild card, as do the three other cards in the deck with that value—so if a four is turned up as a wild card, the other three fours in the deck also become wild. A final round of betting occurs.

ALERT!

When the dealer flips over the outside cards, he must alternate between flipping over a row card and a column card (or vice versa). This adds drama to the rounds of betting, as you don't yet know whether you will use the row or column cards.

Winning/Showdown

If at any time during the betting rounds there is only one person remaining (that is, every other player folds), that player wins and takes the pot. If two or more players remain, those players have reached the showdown and must reveal their hands. If you have the best hand using the cards in your hand, and either a row or column of the cross, you win and take the pot.

Follow the Queen

Follow the Queen, often referred to simply as Queens, is a variation on traditional seven-card stud poker. Although the queens are not wild, they help determine wild cards when they are turned up. The objective of this game is to win money by having the best poker hand. You'll need at least two players and a deck of fifty-two cards.

Follow the Queen opens with all players anteing into the game, and the dealer deals two cards, one at a time, face down, to each player. He then deals the third card (the door card) face up to each player. If a queen shows face up during any part of the deal, the dealer immediately flips the next card up to the center of the table. This becomes a wild card, along with the other three cards of the same rank, for all players. For example, if the dealer turns up an eight following the appearance of a queen, all eights become wild. The dealer continues to deal out the rest of the cards for that round.

Players evaluate their cards, and the one with the highest card showing on the table begins a round of betting. If he doesn't want to make a bet, he folds, and play continues clockwise. When it's your turn, you have the option of folding or matching the bet by paying into the pot. A fourth card is dealt up to all players.

Play and betting occurs around the table twice more, with the dealer dealing one up card to each player before each round. If another queen is turned up on the table, the dealer must flip the next card up, and the first wild card is replaced with this new wild card! Just when you are set to win a game, you're forced to re-evaluate with different cards. The dealer deals a last card face down, and a final round of betting occurs, followed by the remaining players revealing their hands. The highest five-card poker hand wins.

ALERT!

There is one variation in which the queen is also a wild card, whether it's dealt in the face-down or face-up cards. This increases the number of wild cards available to eight, making your hand a good one if you hold any of those cards!

Progressive Rummy

Progressive Rummy is played in a series of hands with varying wild cards. You'll need four to six players and a standard deck of fifty-two cards. The objective of Progressive Rummy is to win points by arranging your eight cards into melds. In the first deal, aces are wild. In the second deal, twos are wild. In the third deal, threes are wild, and so on. After the thirteenth deal, when kings are wild, the first game is considered complete and the player with the fewest points wins.

A random dealer is chosen and deals out eight cards, one at a time, face down, to each player. The dealer turns up the next card, face up, and this begins the discard pile. The remainder of the cards are placed face down next to the discard pile and become the stockpile. Deal continues to alternate after each hand.

Play begins with the first player to the dealer's left. In your turn, you may take the top card in the discard pile or the top card from the stockpile. You may then lay down a meld of three or more cards in a sequence of the same suit (such as 7♥ 8♥ 9♥), or three or more cards of the same value (7♥ 7♠ 7♣). You may also add cards to melds that have already been laid down if you can. There is no minimum or maximum number of cards you can lay down. You end your turn by discarding a card. If a wild card has been played, you may replace that card with its natural card and then use the wild card to complete a meld in your hand that you wish to lay down. Play continues multiple times around the table.

The first player to discard all of his cards ends that hand, and the hand is scored. All players still holding cards add up the points contained in the cards that they hold, not including the melds. Face cards (jack, queen, and king) score ten points each, and the remaining cards score their value. If you hold a wild card for that hand, the wild card is worth twenty points instead of its normal value. The player with the fewest points after the thirteenth hand wins the game.

FACT

To make it easier on the scorekeeper, start off the game by writing A, 2, 3, 4, 5, 6, 7, 8, 9, 10, J, Q, K down the left side of the paper and the names of the players across the top of the paper. This way each player knows what wild-card hand it is, and the scorekeeper can keep track of the scores.

Salt-and-Pepper

No other card game uses as many wild cards as Salt-and-Pepper. The twos, fours, tens, and one-eyed jacks (the J♠ and J♥) are all wild, making fourteen wild cards in all. Salt-and-Pepper is a poker game, and your objective is to win the pot. You'll need two or more players and a deck of fifty-two playing cards. Salt-and-Pepper can be played draw or stud style.

Draw Style

Everyone antes to start the game. The dealer deals five cards, one at a time, face down, to each player. Beginning with the player to the dealer's left, each player can check, bet, or fold his hand. Those players who remain in the game can discard any cards from their hand, to be replaced by the dealer. The player to the dealer's left starts a final round of betting as above. The remaining players show their hands, and the highest hand wins the pot.

Stud Style

Everyone antes to start the game. The dealer deals two cards down and one card face up to each player. The player with the highest card showing on the table begins a round of betting by paying the minimum bet into the pot. If the player doesn't want to bet, he folds, and play continues clockwise. The dealer deals three more up cards, with rounds of betting in between each. If a pair is showing on the table, the minimum bet automatically doubles from that point on. A final card is dealt face down to any player who remains in the game. The player with the highest hand showing begins a final round of betting. Players must match the bet or fold their hands. The remaining players display their hands, and the highest hand wins the pot.

ALERT!

With fourteen wild cards in the game of Salt-and-Pepper, betting wisely is important. Having a hand with a few wild cards won't turn it into a winner. If you think your opponents have you beat, they probably do.

Spit in the Ocean

No spitting takes place in this game, but there is always a bit of drama when one player yells "Spit!" during the deal! Spit in the Ocean is dealt similarly to the other five-card draw games, but with two differences. After you ante, the dealer begins dealing four cards face down to each player, instead of the usual five. During the deal, the first player to shout "Spit!" brings the deal to a halt. At that time, the dealer turns up a single community card to the center of the table. This card becomes the fifth card in each player's hand. The spit card is a wild card, along with the other three cards of the same value.

The player to the dealer's left begins the first round of betting by checking, betting, or folding. The betting round continues around the table, and each player in turn can call the bet, raise the bet, or fold. The players still in the game can then discard up to two of the cards in their hand, to be replaced by the dealer from the deck. The player to the dealer's left then begins a final round of betting. The showdown continues around the table, with all other players matching, raising, or folding. The remaining players then reveal their hands, and the highest hand wins the pot.

Wild Widow

Wild Widow is dealt the same as Spit in the Ocean. After each player antes, the dealer deals four cards face down to each player. He then deals one card face up to the middle of the table. This card is not a community card, but if a player has a card of the same value in his hand, that card becomes wild. The dealer then deals one more card face down to each player.

The player to the dealer's left starts the first betting round by checking, betting, or folding, and play continues around the table until each player has acted. You can then discard cards in your hand, to be replaced by the dealer from the deck. The player to the dealer's left begins a final round of betting as above. This continues around the table, and any remaining players reveal their hands. The highest hand wins the pot.

Chapter 17

Easy Card Games

If you're new to the realm of playing card games, or if you're looking for a quick and easy game to pass the time, you've come to the right chapter. You'll find some fun variations of poker games in Football, Baseball, and Mexican Sweat. Clock is a fun addition to the solitaire family. Michigan and Red Dog are both interesting gambling games that require little skill, just a bit of luck!

Clock

Clock is a solitary game, requiring just one player and a standard deck of fifty-two cards. The objective of Clock is to get all of your cards in their appropriate time slot before capturing all four kings. Shuffle and deal out thirteen stacks of four cards. Starting with the top of your playing field, put one card face down at the twelve o'clock position. Follow that by placing one card face down at the one o'clock position and so on, until you reach the eleven o'clock position. Place a thirteenth card in the center of the circle to form the "hand" of the clock. Repeat this three more times until the deck is entirely used.

ALERT!

Clock requires very little strategy, since there is only one play for every card and you're just manipulating the face of the clock. The shuffle of the deck determines whether you will win or lose, before you even play the game! But watch out, this game can be rather addictive.

Turn up the top card in the clock hand. Move this card to its corresponding time slot (one through ten are, respectively, one through ten o'clock, jacks are eleven o'clock, queens are twelve o'clock, and kings form the clock hand). Place the card face up at the bottom of the pile of its time slot, and take the top card from the same time slot. For instance, you would place a four face up on the bottom of the four o'clock time slot, take the top card from the four o'clock time slot, and move that to its time slot. Move this card to its corresponding time slot and continue play. If a king is turned over, this goes at the bottom of the clock hand, and the top card of the clock hand is played. The game ends when all of the kings are face up and there are no more cards to be taken from the clock hand or when all of the clock times are face up. If the kings are turned up first, you lose. If the clock is turned up first, you win!

Football

Football is a lesser-known, quick-and-easy variation of poker. Football is a stud game and requires two to six players and a standard deck of fifty-two cards. (You can add more players by adding more decks of cards.) Choose a minimum bet before starting the game. Each player antes that minimum bet before play begins.

Rules of Play

Football kicks off with the dealer dealing, one at a time, two cards face down and one card face up to each player. The deal will move to the left with each hand played. The player with the highest card face up begins a round of betting. If two players each show the same high card, the one closest to the dealer's left starts the round. He must check or make a bet, and the betting round continues to the left. Once everyone has acted, the dealer deals a second card face up to the players still in the game. Fours and sixes are wild, but if you are dealt a four face up, you must match the pot by placing an equal amount of money from your hand, or drop from the game. The player whose up cards give him the highest hand (a pair or a high single card) leads a second round of betting. The dealer deals a third face up card, followed by a round of betting, and deals a fourth face-up card, followed by another round of betting. If you are dealt a two face up during any of the four rounds, you are given an additional face down card that you can view and add to your hand. If you are dealt a two face down, you don't gain an additional card.

The Final Score

The dealer finally deals one last card face down to each player. The player showing the best hand on the table with her four up cards begins a final round of betting. Once all players have acted, they turn over their cards in a showdown. The best five-card poker hand (formed out of seven— or more if you were dealt a two face up—cards) wins. If at any time during the game there is only one player remaining, he wins the pot, and a new hand is dealt.

Baseball

Baseball is a close relative of Football and is also an easy and enjoyable poker variation. You'll need two to six players and a standard deck of fifty-two cards to play. Before you begin, agree on a minimum bet. Each player antes to the pot to start the first "inning" and play of the game.

Rules of Play

The dealer deals two cards face down and one card face up to each player. The player with the highest up card begins a round of betting. (If two players each show the same high card, the one closest to the dealer's left starts the round.) Each player must act by checking, betting, raising, or folding. Once everyone has acted, the dealer deals a second card face up to the players still in the game.

ALERT!

In one variation of Baseball, if the Q♠ is turned up, the game is considered a rainout and the hand is over. Every player re-antes to the pot, doubling the pot size, and a new hand is dealt. You don't want to see the Q♠ if you hold a good poker hand, but she's a great card if you've already folded!

The player with the highest hand in his two face-up cards leads a second round of betting. The dealer deals a third face-up card, followed by a round of betting, and a fourth face-up card, followed by another round of betting. The dealer finally deals one last card face down to each player. The player showing the best hand on the table with his four face-up cards begins a final round of betting. Once all players have played, they turn over their cards in a showdown. The best five-card poker hand wins and takes the pot.

The Wild Cards

In the game of Baseball, threes and nines are wild, but if you are dealt a wild card face up, you must match the pot by adding money from your pool, or drop from the game. If you are dealt a four face up during any of the four rounds, you are given an additional face-down card that you can view and add to your hand. If you are dealt a four face down, you don't gain an additional card.

Mexican Sweat

This easy and enjoyable variation on poker is played without wild cards. It is played with two to seven players and a standard deck of fifty-two cards. The objective, like all poker games, is to win money by betting strategically. There's no bluffing in Mexican Sweat because the players get to see your cards. Players should agree on a minimum bet, which is also the amount of the ante.

Each player antes, then the dealer deals seven cards face down to each player. Players may not look at their cards. If any player does look, she must match the pot as a penalty. The first player to the left of the dealer starts by turning over his top card. This first card shown automatically becomes the highest card. A round of betting occurs, in which each player pays the minimum into the pot. Since the first player turns up a card, and everyone must immediately add the minimum bet to the pot, you can choose to ante twice the minimum bet and forgo this round of betting to speed up play.

Once the betting is complete, the next player turns up his top card. If this card is higher than the previous player's, play stops and a second round of betting takes place, where each player can bet, check, raise, or fold. If this card is lower in value, the player turns another card beside the first, and so on until the hand beats the previous player's card. If, during the roll, the player turns up a pair or better, the minimum bet doubles for all players.

For example, if the previous high card was a ten and you turn over a jack, you stop and a round of betting occurs. If you turn up a nine, you continue turning over cards until you turn over one card that is higher than a ten, or you turn over another nine. You would then stop, and a round of betting would occur.

If the next player turns up all of his cards and cannot beat the previous player's hand, his turn is over, and the player to his left starts turning over his cards. No betting takes place in between turns. Either way, play continues to the next player clockwise and he has to beat the previous high hand showing on the table. For example, once a pair is shown, it has to be beaten by a higher pair, or a higher poker hand of two pair, three of a kind, and so on.

Play continues around the table to the dealer and back to the player on the dealer's left, with each player rolling his cards up to beat the hand that came before him. The game ends when all the players have rolled up their cards or when there is only one player left in the game holding the highest five-card poker hand. Play continues until all players but one have folded their cards or turned up all of their cards. The final player standing is the winner.

FACT

Rolling is when you turn up a stack of face-down cards, one at a time, for all other players to see. Rolling occurs most often in games of poker like this one, but you also see it in the kids' game War.

The variation of Midnight Baseball, or Murder, is a combination of Baseball and Mexican Sweat. The deal and play is the same as Mexican Sweat, but the wild cards and structure in Baseball are added to make the game a bit more interesting.

Michigan

Also known as Chicago, Boodle, Newmarket, and Stops, this game is very simple to learn and is a great icebreaker for players who do not know one another. You'll need three to eight players, a set of poker chips, a standard deck of fifty-two cards, and a jack, queen, king, and ace (all of different suits) from another pack of cards. Aces rank high, and twos rank low. You'll place the jack, queen, king, and ace from the second deck in the middle of the table, side by side and face up. These are called the boodle cards. The objective is to be the first player to discard all of your cards and also to collect chips by playing a boodle card (described later). You should establish a value for the poker chips so that each chip is of equal value. (In other words, you only need dollar chips, not a selection including $1, $5, and $10 chips.)

Each player must place the agreed-upon ante on a combination of any or all of the boodle cards. You can divide up your ante equally, put it all on one boodle card, or however you would like to arrange it.

A random dealer is selected, and he deals out all of the cards to the deck, one at a time, including an extra hand to his left. This hand will not be seen by any of the players. The player to the left of the dealer starts playing by laying down the lowest card in any of his suits. If you have the next card in sequence in the same suit, you play that card, no matter where at the table you sit. This continues with players playing their cards one at a time in order, until a card is not available (because it is in the extra hand) or when the sequence reaches an ace. When the play stops, the last player to play before the stop leads the next hand. He must play the lowest card in a new suit. If he does not have a card in a new suit, he passes the lead to the player on his left. Play ends with the first player to discard all of his cards. If you go out first, you get to collect one chip from each player for every card that he holds in his hand.

So what about the boodle cards?
If at any time you play a card that is the same as one of the boodle cards, you collect the chips on that card. If the game ends before the chips are taken off a card, those chips remain for the next hand.

QUESTION?

Red Dog

Red Dog is a game in which each player plays against the dealer, so any number of players can play. Depending on the number of players, you'll use one or more decks of fifty-two cards (a six-deck game is standard). Cards with values from two to ten count as their face value, jacks have a value of eleven, queens are twelve, kings are thirteen, and aces are fourteen. Suits do not matter. The objective in Red Dog is to bet correctly on the value of the third card that is dealt, betting on whether it falls in between the values of the first two cards.

Rules of Play

Each player places a bet in the spot marked "Bet" if playing on a Red Dog table (similar to a blackjack table). Otherwise, you just place a bet in front of you on a standard table. After all bets have been laid, the dealer deals two cards face up in front of him, placing one on the right and one on the left. The dealer then places a marker on the table. This mark indicates the spread between the two cards (the number of cards with values between the two cards showing), and the odds the house offers on that spread (page 205). If you do not play on a Red Dog table, you might wish to have a paper with the spread and odds available.

The spread between the two cards does not include the value of the cards. For example, if the first card is a six and the second card is a queen, the spread is five (the seven, eight, nine, ten, and jack).

Payout

If the dealer's first two cards are a pair, he turns over a third card. If that card is of the same value as the first two, you receive an eleven-to-one payout. If it does not match in value, it's a push, and you get back your money. If the two cards are in a consecutive value (such as a two and a three), it's also a push, and you get back your money. If there is a spread between the two cards, you have a chance to increase your bet by putting in more money and moving the bet from the bet field to the raise field on the table. If you do not raise the bet, you stand on your original bet.

The dealer draws a third card, and if it is outside the range of the two cards, or it makes a pair with either card, you lose your bets. If it is between the two original cards, you win as follows:

- One-card spread has a 5:1 payout
- Two-card spread has a 4:1 payout
- Three-card spread has a 2:1 payout
- Four-plus card spread has a 1:1 payout

When determining if you want to raise your bet, you'll want to know the probability of winning that spread. In a six-deck game, the probability is as follows.

Probability in Red Dog of Winning the Spread

Spread	Probability	Spread	Probability
1	0.077	7	0.542
2	0.155	8	0.619
3	0.232	9	0.697
4	0.310	10	0.774
5	0.387	11	0.852
6	0.465		

The player's odds become favorable with a spread of seven or greater, so you should raise your bet if the spread is higher than six. On a spread of six or less, stand on your bet.

Chapter 18

Complex Card Games

Now that you've mastered some easier card games, it's time to advance to the games that require a lot of skill, concentration, and unfortunately, in most cases, extensive rules! Complex card games typically take awhile to play, but are a great way to pass the time with a good group of friends. Anaconda and baccarat are both gambling games, while Calypso, Sheepshead, and Skat are trick-taking games.

Anaconda

Anaconda is a seven-card stud poker game sometimes referred to as "Pass the Trash" because players pass their worst cards over to the player on their left. The objective of the game is to win money in the pot. There are eight rounds of betting, so be prepared for large pots and long games if everyone stays in! Anaconda can be played with two to seven players using a standard pack of fifty-two cards.

Rules of Play

Select a dealer, who deals seven cards face down to each player. The first step of play is a round of betting, beginning with the player to the dealer's left. Each player may check, bet, raise, or fold. After each player has acted, those of you still in the game each pass three cards from your hand to the player on your left. A second round of betting occurs, starting with the player to the dealer's left. If more than one player remains after all bets have been called, you each pass two cards to the player on your left. A third round of betting occurs, starting with the player to the dealer's left. If more than one player remains, you each pass one last card to the player on your left. A fourth round of betting takes place.

E ALERT!

With so many rounds of betting, it's hard to know when to get out of the game. If you have a great hand of five cards after the first round of betting, you can keep those cards in your hand and pass the other two cards in the second and third rounds. Otherwise, you might want to get out quickly!

If there are two or more players left in the game after these four rounds of betting, you each create your best poker hand of five cards. You place this hand in a stack in front of you, face down, and discard the other two cards from your hand. The dealer says "one, two, three, flip" and you each flip over the top card in your stack. A fifth round of betting occurs, now led by the player who shows the highest card. This process is repeated with the second, third, and fourth card in the stack being turned over followed by a round of betting. The player to start those betting rounds is the player with the highest hand in the cards showing (the highest single card, highest pair, and so on). When the fifth card is turned over, your entire hand is revealed, and the winner is determined. The player with the best five-card poker hand wins the pot. If at any time during the game there is only one player remaining during a round of betting, he wins and takes the pot.

Variations

There are a few different variations of Anaconda. You can choose the option called "pass in progression" if you are playing with four or more players. In this game, you pass your first set of cards to the first person on your left, your second set of cards to the second player on your left, and your third set of cards to the third player on your left. In the variation called Bisexual, in the first round you pass two cards to the player on your left and then two cards to the player on your right. In the second round you pass one card to the player on your right and then one card to the player on your left. When playing Love Thy Neighbor, you split your earnings with the player on your right (or the player on your left, as long as this is decided before playing the hand) if you win the game.

Baccarat

The game of baccarat is believed to have originated in Italy. It was introduced to the French Court in the fifteenth century and became the favorite game among French nobility. Any number of players can play. The player's objective is to get a hand that is closer to the value of nine than the hand that the banker is dealt. A standard pack of fifty-two cards is used, with no wild cards. In casinos, it is typical to use six or eight decks. Aces are worth one point, twos are worth two points, and so on. Tens and face cards count as ten points. If your hand goes over ten, you must subtract ten to get a value between zero and nine, and therefore tens are actually worth zero points.

Dealing the Hand

Baccarat is played with only one player (typically the player who placed the highest bet) and the banker, but any number of players can bet on the game. In some casinos the dealer is a player and the banker, while in other casinos the dealer remains the same and the banker rotates among the players. The first banker is the person to the dealer's right, or in some cases the player with the most money.

There are three bets that you can place in Baccarat. You can bet on the player, on the bank, or on a tie between the player and the bank. The banker is not required to bet on the bank—he can bet on the player or a tie if he chooses. After all bets have been placed, the dealer deals two cards, face down, to the participant and the banker. The participant looks at his cards and hands them back to the dealer, who turns them over and declares the card value. The banker views his hand, passes it back to the dealer, and his hand is also declared.

The Rules

If either hand has a natural (a value of eight or nine), that hand automatically wins. If neither hand has a natural, the player has two options: add a card or stand. If you hold a total of six or seven, you should stand. You should draw a card if you have a total of four or below. With a total of five, you have a choice of standing or drawing, although experts recommend drawing.

The Rules for the Dealer	
Banker's Total	Banker Should . . .
7–9	Stand
6	Draw if player has 6 or 7
5	Draw if player has 4–7
4	Draw if player has 2–7
3	Draw if player has 0–7 or 9
0–2	Draw no matter what

A tie of nines or eights is a push, but a natural (a value of eight or nine with only two cards) beats a three-card hand. After the two hands have been compared, the banker pays out and collects bets around the table for all those players who have bet. Another hand is dealt after any players choose to ante and play again.

When you bet on the player and win, you receive an amount equal to your bet. When you bet on the bank and win, you receive an amount equal to your bet minus a 5-percent commission. When you bet on a tie and win, you receive an amount equal to nine times your bet.

FACT

Baccarat is typically played in casinos with cash instead of chips. The table is usually roped off from the majority of games and spectators, allowing high-rollers to play their large bills with some degree of normalcy.

Calypso

The objective of Calypso is to score points by building suit stacks, called calypsos, from ace to king in your own trump suit. This game can get complicated because each player has his own trump suit. Don't forget to pay attention when your opponents throw down their cards. The game is typically played with four people in two teams, with partners sitting across the table from one another. You'll use four standard packs of fifty-two cards, with aces high and twos low.

Choosing Your Trump

Calypso opens with each player cutting one deck to determine individual trumps and seats. The player with the highest card picks his chair and his trump. His partner takes the seat and trump opposite him. Spades and hearts are partners and diamonds and clubs are partners. The dealer shuffles all four decks together and deals thirteen cards to each player.

Playing the Tricks

The player to the dealer's left plays his first card, laying down any card from his hand. Play continues clockwise around the table. When it's your turn, you must follow suit if possible, or otherwise play another card from your hand. The winner of the hand is the player who plays the highest card in the trick led, who plays his trump, or who overtrumps by playing a higher card in his own trump. The exception is if someone leads with a card from his own trump. He automatically wins the trick even if another player plays a higher card in that suit, unless another player trumps or overtrumps. If two players lay identical trump card values, the first card wins and that player has the advantage. If two players lay identical cards, the first beats the second unless the second player to lay down is playing a card from his own trump. For instance, if the player before you lays down a 10♣ and you also lay down a 10♣, he beats you unless clubs is your trump suit. Your goal in winning these tricks is to obtain cards in your own trump suit to build calypsos.

ALERT!

When you lead a card that is not your trump (if you lead a Q♣ when your trump is spades), the player who has that trump suit (clubs in this example) does not win by playing a club, even though it is his trump suit. Otherwise every hand would have a trump! He may only win a trick by playing a club when a suit other than clubs is led.

Building Calypsos

When you win a trick, you take any cards from that trick that will help you build your calypso. A calypso is a suit stack (ace to king) in your trump suit. You may only build one calypso at a time, so if you already have a four in your trump suit, and you win another four (since you're using multiple decks of cards), you must discard it. You keep your calypso stack in front of you, easily accessible for adding cards. After you take any cards that help you to build your calypso, you may pass any cards that help your partner build his calypso. You then discard the remaining cards. When you complete one calypso, you may start a second, but you may not use any of your discarded cards to help build it.

After the first thirteen tricks have been played, the player to the dealer's left deals the next thirteen cards without shuffling the deck. Play continues with you building on your original calypsos until each player has dealt and the four decks have been played through.

Scoring the Game

After all the tricks have been played, each player wins 500 points for his first calypso, 750 points for his second calypso, and 1,000 points for any third or fourth calypsos. You also win twenty points for each card in an incomplete calypso and ten points for each card in your discard pile. You and your partner add your totals together and compare them to your opponent's combined score. The team with the most points subtracts their opponents' points, and the difference between those scores becomes the final score of the winning team.

Sheepshead

Sheepshead is an old middle-European card game that was developed by shepherds in the late 1700s. Sheepshead also goes by the name Schafkopf (German for "sheepshead") or Shep and is similar in play to pinochle and euchre. With a challenging rule system, this game rewards those diligent enough to learn it. You can play Sheepshead with two to eight players although it's most commonly played with three to five. If there are three or four players, they play for themselves, and if there are five players, they play in teams. The objective of Sheepshead is to win the most points by bidding and taking tricks with high-value cards. You'll use a shortened deck of thirty-two cards with the seven through the ace of each suit.

The Value of Cards

The four queens and the four jacks make up the top eight trumps. They rank as Q♣ Q♠ Q♥ Q♦ J♣ J♠ J♥ J♦. The next highest in rank are the diamonds, which make up a suit of trumps—A♦ 10♦ K♦ 9♦ 8♦ 7♦. The other suits are equal in value, and the cards rank high to low in the same order.

The cards also have values associated with them. The ace is worth eleven, the ten is worth ten, the king is worth four, the queen is worth three, the jack is worth two, and the remaining three cards are worth zero. So even though the queens and jacks help you take tricks, they are worth fewer points than tens and aces.

FACT

It is suggested that the ranking of cards for taking tricks in Sheepshead is structured thus because the peasants at the time were unhappy with royalty. They chose to make the queens and jacks have a higher rank and beat out the kings.

Dealing the Cards

Sheepshead opens with a random dealer being selected. When it's your turn to deal, deal a group of three cards to each player, face down. Place two cards face down in the middle of the table to form the "blind" which will be used in the next stage of play. Then deal another group of three cards to each player, face down. Deal passes to the left with each hand.

Picking the Blind

The player to the left of the dealer has the option to pick the blind. By picking up the blind, a player declares that she will win at least sixty-one points in captured cards during the hand. If she does not wish to take the blind, she says, "Pass." If all players pass, the game is considered a misdeal, and that hand is over. (In one variation of Sheepshead, if all players pass, the game is a "leaster," and the object is to take the fewest points. In order to qualify to win, you must win at least one trick. The winner receives a point from each player.)

If you're the first player to pick up the blind, you become the "picker" or declarer. You add the two cards to your hand and discard two cards from those you were already holding. These cards will count toward your points at the end of the game, but they will not be used in play. If there are three or four players, you play by yourself. If there are five players, as the declarer you can go alone against the other players or "choose" a partner by declaring one of the nontrump suits. You must have at least one card in that suit, but it cannot be the ace. If you discard an ace after picking up the blind, you may not call that suit. The player who has the ace of that suit becomes your partner, but he does not say it out loud. You will not know who your partner is until he plays the ace on a trick.

ALERT!

Another variation of Sheepshead is that the holder of the J♦ is automatically the declarer's partner. The partner lets himself be known by playing the jack at the first time a trump card can be played.

Playing the Hand

The player to the dealer's left leads the first card by playing any one card from his hand. Play continues clockwise around the table. When it's your turn, you must follow suit if possible by playing one card from your hand in that suit. If you cannot, you may play any card from your hand. The player with the highest card in the suit led, or the highest trump, wins the trick and leads the next trick. When all six hands have been played, add up the points in the cards you have won based on their values given earlier.

In a five-player game, the hand is scored as follows. If you are the declarer and win a combined value of sixty-one points or more with your partner, you receive two points, and your partner receives one point. Each of your opponents loses one point. If your team wins a combined value of sixty points or fewer, you lose two points, your partner loses one point, and your opponents each receive one point.

In a four-player game, the hand is scored as follows. If you are the declarer and win a value of at least sixty-one points, you receive three points, and each of your opponents loses one point. If you win a value fewer than sixty-one points, you lose three points, and your opponents each receive one point.

In a three-player game, the hand is scored as follows. If you're the declarer and win a value of at least sixty-one points, you receive two points, and your opponents lose one point each. If you win a value fewer than sixty-one points, you lose two points and your opponents each receive one point.

In all instances, if one team or player wins ninety-one points or more in one hand, the hand is a "Schneider" and the points are doubled. If one side or player wins all the tricks, the hand is a "Schwarz" and the points are tripled. The player with the most points after ten hands wins the game.

The declarer theoretically has more trump than his opponents, since he picked the blind on a good hand. By leading trump, the declarer can usually draw out five trump cards, leaving only nine in all hands.

Skat

Skat was developed in 1811 in Altenburg, Germany, and today is the national card game in that country. It is played with three players. The objective of skat is to win the most points by bidding and winning tricks with high-value cards. Like Sheepshead, skat uses a shortened deck of thirty-two cards with the seven through the ace in each suit.

The Value of Cards

The ranking of the cards depends on the game the declarer chooses to play after winning the bidding process (described below). If the declarer chooses a suit game, the four jacks are the top four trumps, no matter what suit is picked as trump. They rank as J♣ J♠ J♥ J♦. The next highest in rank are the seven cards in the trump suit in the order of ace, ten, king, queen, nine, eight, and seven. The other suits are equal, and the cards rank high to low in the same order. If the declarer chooses a grand game, the four jacks are the only trumps and rank in order from J♣ J♠ J♥ J♦. The four suits are all equal, and the cards rank from high to low as ace, ten, king, queen, nine, eight, and seven. If the declarer chooses a null game, there are no trumps, the four suits are all equal, and the cards rank in each suit from high to low as ace, king, queen, jack, ten, nine, eight, and seven.

When playing suit and grand games, the cards each have values. The jack is worth two, the ace is worth eleven, the ten is worth ten, the king is worth four, the queen is worth three, and the remaining three cards are worth zero. The total value of the cards is 120 points.

Dealing the Cards

Skat opens with a random dealer being selected and dealing a group of three cards face down to each player, a group of four cards face down to each player, and a final group of three cards face down to each player. The remaining two cards are placed face down on the table and form the "skat," which will be used below. In the game of skat, the dealer is called Rearhand (or Posthand), the player to his left is called Forehand, and the player to his right is called Middlehand. Deal rotates to the left for each hand.

Bidding the Hand

After the cards have been dealt, you pick up your cards and determine if you want to bid for a suit, grand, or null. Each bid is equal to a possible value that can be taken in a game of suit, grand, or null. Bidding a number means you are prepared to play and take that many points. The explanation of scoring is below, but the possible values to be bid are 18, 20, 22, 23, 24, 27, 30, 33, 35, 36, 40, 44, 45, 46, 48, 50, and so on.

Middlehand starts by bidding with Forehand. As Middlehand, you can either pass or make a minimum bid of eighteen points. If you do place a bid, Forehand can either say "Pass" or compete for the bid by saying "Yes." If Forehand says "Yes," you can either say "Pass" or say a higher bid, turning the bidding back to Forehand. This continues until one of you passes. The bidding then moves to include Rearhand and takes place in the same fashion with the winner of the previous bidding. As the junior player, Rearhand must bid higher than the previous bid or pass the hand. If he bids higher, the other players can compete for the bid or pass. The winning bidder becomes the "soloist," and the other two players become the "defensive" partners. If all three of you pass, the cards are thrown in, and the deal passes to the player on the left for a new hand.

Playing the Tricks

After the bidding is over, if you're the soloist, you must determine if you want to pick up the two skat cards to see if they add value to your hand. If you do, the game is a skat game; otherwise, you're playing a hand game. If you picked up the skat cards, you must discard two cards so that your total hand still has ten cards. You must then announce the game by saying it is a grand game, null game, or suit game and declare the trump suit. If you choose grand or a suit game, your goal is to take at least sixty-one points in playing the tricks. If you choose null, your goal is to lose every trick. If you opt to play null ouvert (open null), your goal is to lose every trick, but all of your cards are exposed to your opponents. If you have not looked at the skat cards, you can also choose one of three points to increase the value of the game. You can say "Schneider," which means your goal is to win at least ninety points, "Schwarz," which means your goal is to take all of the tricks, or "ouvert," which means your goal is to win all the tricks with your cards exposed.

The player to the dealer's left then leads the first card by placing it face up on the table. Play continues to the left and each player plays a card. The player with the highest card in the suit led, or the highest trump, wins the trick. If either of the defensive partners wins the trick, it goes in a communal pile. The soloist keeps his own pile in front of him. The winner of the trick leads the next one. When all ten hands have been played, the players add up their points, and a new hand is played.

Scoring the Hand

To obtain the value of a suit or grand game, multiply together the base value and the multiplier as follows:

Suit	Base Value
Diamonds	9
Hearts	10
Spades	11
Clubs	12
Grand	24

The multiplier is obtained by adding up any values applicable as follows:

Multiplier	Skat Game	Hand Game
Matadors (with or against)	1 per	1 per
Game	1	1
Hand	0	1
Schneider	1	1
Schneider announced	0	1
Schwarz	1	1
Schwarz announced	0	1
Open	0	1

The matadors are the J♣ and an unbroken sequence of top trumps. If you are the soloist and have a matador plus the skat, you are "with" that number of matadors. If the opponents have a matador in their combined hand, the soloist is "against" that number of matadors. The game point is just a standard point added in.

For example, you are the soloist and declared a suit game with hearts as the trump. You looked at the two skat cards, you had the J♣ and J♠ as matadors, and you won ninety-one points. The multiplier value would be 2 matadors + 1 game + 1 Schneider + 0 Schneider announced + 0 Schwarz + 0 Schwarz announced + 0 open = 4 multipliers. This is multiplied by the base value of ten for hearts, and the game is valued at forty points.

Here's another example. Say you are the soloist and declared a grand game. You did not look at the two skat cards, you announced Schneider, your opponents had the J♣ as a matador, and you won all the tricks. The multiplier value would be 1 matador + 1 game + 1 Schneider + 1 Schneider announced + 1 Schwarz + 0 Schwarz announced + 0 Open = 5 multipliers. This is multiplied by the base value of twenty-four for grand, and the game is valued at 120 points.

The minimum possible value of a game is eighteen points, because the minimum multipliers are two (one for game and one matador) and the minimum base value is nine for diamonds. So the minimum game is a suit game with diamonds as trump.

If the soloist declares a null game, the value is as follows:

Bid	Value
Null	23
Null hand	35
Null ouvert	46
Null ouvert hand	59

If you are the soloist and win your game and at least as many points as the value of your bid, you receive points equal to the value of the game. If you lose the game by making less than the value of your bid, you lose points equal to double the value of the game. If you announce Schneider but take fewer than ninety card points, or if you announced Schwarz or open and lost a trick, you lose and count the multipliers that you would have won with the tricks available. At the end of an agreed-upon number of games, with each player having dealt an equal amount of times, the player with the highest total score wins.

Chapter 19

E Card Games from Other Lands

Card games from different countries can introduce you to new terminology, variations on games that you're used to playing, or different scoring and bonus structures. You can even learn a little about that country's culture based on the name of the game, terms used during play, and how the cards are ranked. This chapter teaches you some of the popular games played in lands across the globe.

Black Maria (Britain)

Black Maria is the British version of the game hearts. It also goes by the names Black Lady, Dirty Lady, Black Widow, Slippery Anne, and Slippery Bitch. The objective of Black Maria is to get rid of your cards without capturing the queen of spades (the Black Maria) or any hearts. The game is typically played with three players, although it can be played with anywhere from three to seven people. You'll need a standard deck of fifty-two cards to play. For three players, remove the 2♣; for five players, remove the 2♣ and 2♦; for six players, remove all of the twos; and for seven players, remove all of the twos except the 2♥.

Dealing the Hand

Black Maria opens with a random dealer being selected. When it's your turn to deal, deal out the entire deck, one a time, face down to the players and yourself. If there are three players, you will each receive seventeen cards. If you're playing a game with four players, you will each receive thirteen cards. Five players will receive ten cards each. Six players will receive eight cards each. Seven players will receive seven cards each. Deal will alternate clockwise with each hand played.

Playing the Tricks

Play begins with the players exchanging cards. With three or four players, you each select three cards from your hand. With five or more players, you each select two cards from your hand. You then pass those cards to the player on your right, meaning you receive the cards from the player on your left. The player to the dealer's left leads the first trick and may play any one card from his hand, including a heart. Play continues clockwise around the table. When it's your turn, you must follow suit if you're able by playing one card from your hand in the suit led. If you cannot follow suit, you must play another card from your hand. The player with the highest card in the suit led wins the trick and leads the next one. Your goal at this time is to avoid taking a trick with hearts or with the Black Maria. When all of the cards have been played, the hand is over.

Scoring

Each heart is worth one point, and the Black Maria is worth thirteen points. The exception to this is if you collect all of the hearts and the Black Maria in your hand. Then you score zero points, and your opponents each score twenty-six points. When a player reaches fifty points, the game is over and the player with the lowest score wins.

FACT

One scoring variation includes adding ten points for the K♠ and seven points for the A♠. Another variation counts each heart at its face value (with face cards worth ten points each and the ace worth fifteen), and the Black Maria is worth twenty-five points.

Klaverjas (Greenland)

Klaverjas is played with four or more players who form two teams, with partners sitting across from one another. The objective of Klaverjas is to score points through taking tricks. You'll use a shortened deck of thirty-two cards—the ace, king, queen, jack, ten, nine, eight, and seven of each suit. In a nontrump suit, the order of cards ranks from high to low as ace, ten, king, queen, jack, nine, eight, and seven. An ace is worth eleven points, tens are worth ten points, kings are worth four points, queens are worth three points, jacks are worth two points, and the nine, eight, and seven are zero points. In a trump suit, the order of cards in value from high to low is jack, nine, ace, ten, king, queen, eight, and seven. In the trump suit, jacks are worth twenty points, nines are worth fourteen points, aces are worth eleven points, kings are worth four points, queens are worth three points, and the eight and seven are worth zero points.

Rules of Play

A random dealer is selected and deals clockwise a group of three cards, a group of two cards, and a final group of three cards, all face down to each player. The dealer starts a round of bidding to declare the trump suit. He may pass or say "I play . . ." and declare what suit he wants as trump. If he passes, play continues to the left. When it's your turn, you may play or pass. If you all pass, the dealer must declare trump. By choosing a trump, you are stating that during the game you will try to take more points than your opponents, or you risk losing all of the points you earned in that hand.

FACT

You can signal strengths in your hand in Klaverjas by throwing cards out during play. If you discard a low card, it means you hold the ace. If you play one color, it means you are strong in the other suit of that color. If you play a face card, it tells your partner not to lead that suit.

Regardless of who chooses trump, the player to the dealer's left leads the first trick by playing one card from his hand. Play continues around the table. At your turn, you must follow the suit of the card led, if you can, by playing one card of the same suit from your hand. If you do not have a card of that suit, you may play any other card. The player to play the highest card of the suit led, according to the rankings, or the highest trump wins the trick and leads the next one. There are two sets of rules regarding trumps, depending on which game you play. In the Amsterdam variation, if you cannot follow suit and an opponent is winning the trick, you must play a higher trump than is visible on the table, if you have one. If you do not have the cards to overtrump, you must throw away a card from another suit. However, if your partner is winning the trick, you can play a card from any suit, but you cannot undertrump unless you only have cards in the trump suit. If a trump was led, you must play a higher trump if you have it, regardless of who is winning the trick. In the Rotterdam variation, if you cannot follow suit, you must always play a higher trump, if you have one. Play continues until all the cards are gone.

Scoring the Hand

While playing the hand, you can receive bonus points for collecting a trick containing a combination of cards, as follows:

- **Three cards in sequence in the same suit**—20 bonus points
- **Four cards in sequence in the same suit**—50 bonus points
- **King and queen in the trump suit**—20 bonus points
- **Three cards in sequence in the same suit, including the king and queen of trump**—40 bonus points
- **Four cards in sequence in the same suit, including the king and queen of trump**—70 bonus points
- **Four kings, queens, aces, or tens**—100 bonus points
- **Four jacks**—200 bonus points

In order to claim the bonus points, you must call the combination (or roem) when picking up the trick. You also win ten bonus points if you take the last trick, and 100 bonus points if you take all tricks.

At the end of the hand, you each add up the points in your tricks and any bonus points. If your team chose trump and has more points than your opponents, each team wins the points earned. If your team has fewer points than your opponents, you score zero, and your opponents get both sets of points. The team with the highest score after sixteen hands wins the game.

Marjapussi (Finland)

Marjapussi is quite a popular game in Finland. It is played with four players forming two teams (or parties), with partners sitting across from each other. Your objective during play is to score points through taking tricks in order to be the first team to reach 500 points. You'll play with a shortened deck of thirty-six cards (the ace, king, queen, jack, ten, nine, eight, seven, and six in the four standard suits).

The cards rank in order from high to low as ace, ten, king, queen, jack, nine, eight, seven, and six. The ace is worth eleven points, the ten is worth ten points, the king is worth four points, the queen is worth three points, the jack is worth two points, and the nine, eight, seven, and six are worth zero points.

Scoring Points

There are three ways to earn points during play. Card points are the total value of the cards in your hand at the end of play. There are a maximum of 120 card points available. Trump points are earned if your team holds the king and queen in the trump suit (hearts are worth 100 points, diamonds are worth 80 points, clubs are worth 60 points, and spades are worth 40 points). Finally, the team to win the last trick wins an additional 20 points.

ALERT!

The king and queen of the same suit are called a "pair," and a single king or queen of a suit is called a "half." In order to call a trump suit, your team will need to hold the king and queen, either by you holding a pair or by you each holding a half.

Dealing the Hand

Each player cuts the deck to determine their partners. The player who cut the highest card chooses his seat at the table, with the player who cut the lowest card becoming his partner and sitting across from him. The player who cut the highest card becomes the first dealer. He deals out nine cards, one at a time, face down, to each player. The deal passes to the left with each hand.

A Round of Bidding

The player to the dealer's left opens a round of bidding. He may pass or start the bidding at 120 points (indicating the number of points he believes that he and his partner can earn during play). The player to his left may in turn pass or bid higher than the previous bid, in increments of five. If you pass, you may no longer enter in the bidding process. If all players pass, there is no exchange of cards as described later, and no contract to be fulfilled. The contract is the number of points that you will attempt to win while playing the tricks. If a bid is called, the bidding continues until three players pass. The high bidder becomes the declarer. The declarer's partner may choose to pass four cards to the declarer, and the declarer must then return four cards to his partner. After the exchange, the declarer announces his contract, which must be a number of points at least equal to his high bid or higher by an increment of five.

If you're the declarer, and you win your contract, you only receive points equal to your bid. So if you think you can win more points than your high bid, it pays to raise your bid for your final contract.

Rules of Play

The declarer leads the first trick, or, if there is no declarer, the player to the dealer's right leads the first trick. He must begin the first trick by playing an ace. If he doesn't have an ace, he must play a spade. If he has no ace or spade, he may play any card in his hand. Play continues around the table. At the beginning of the hand there is no trump suit, so each player must follow suit if he can, and he must always try to beat the highest card on the table. Otherwise, he may play any card in his hand. The winner of each trick leads the next one. Any tricks played after the first hand may be led with any suit and any value.

If your team holds a queen and king of one suit, you may call that suit as trump after you win a trick and before you play a card to the next trick. You are not obligated to call trump at any time. You can change the suit of trump at any time, as long as you announce it after winning a trick, and as long as you or your partner holds the king and queen in that suit as well. Your opponents can change the trump following the same rules.

You can only announce each trump suit once, and you may not alternate between trump suits after a trump suit has been changed. This is true whether it is your team or your opponents who change the suits.

You may ask your partner during play if she holds a pair or a half in her hand by asking one of the following questions: "Do you have a pair?" or "Do you have a half of ___?" and name the suit you are looking for. Your partner must answer "No" if she does not have the pair or half, and she must answer "Yes" if she does. If she has the pair, that suit becomes trump. If she has the half and you have the other half, that suit becomes trump. If she has the half but you do not have the other half, you declare this and just lead to the next trick. You may only ask one question or declare one trump per trick that you win. Once you ask about a particular suit, you may not ask about that suit again, although your partner may ask you about it if she wins a hand. If you ask your partner about a suit, you cannot on the next trick name a trump yourself. You must wait until at least the next hand to declare a trump if you ask your partner about a suit. Play continues until all cards have been played.

Doubling the Hand

If the opponents think the declarer will fail to make her contract, they can say "Contra" (or "Kontra") when they hold nine cards, doubling the value of the declarer's contract. If you still believe that you will make your contract, you may double the value of your contract again by saying "Re" when you have eight cards. Double your hand only if you are positive you can win! Your opponents may double again when they have seven cards by saying "Contra," and you may double again when you have six cards by saying "Re." This can continue until the end of the game, with a maximum of nine doubles if each team chooses to redouble in each hand.

End of the Game

If you are the declarer and your team scores enough points to win your contract, you add the value of your contract to your score. If you do not win your contract, you subtract the value of your contract from your score. In either case, your opponents score as many points as they earned during play. Points are always rounded up or down to the nearest five. If, as the declarer, your team scores no tricks during play, you get double your contract value subtracted from your score. If your opponents score no tricks during play, but you win your contract, you score your normal contract value, and they must subtract double your contract value from their score (only the original contract value if the hand was doubled via contra or re). If your opponents score no tricks during play, but you do not win your contract, you subtract the value of your contract from your score, and your opponents get no penalty. The first team to reach 500 points wins the game.

P'Yanitsa (Russia)

P'Yanitsa is Russian for "drunkard" and is similar to the game of War. It is typically played with two players, although it is possible to play with three or four. Depending on which version you are playing, the objective of P'Yanitsa is either to get rid of all of your cards or to collect all of the cards. You'll need a shortened deck of thirty-six cards with the ace, king, queen, jack, ten, nine, eight, seven, and six of each suit.

P'Yanitsa opens with the dealer dealing out the entire deck to each player, face-down. Players make a neat stack of their cards and place it in front of them. Simultaneously, you each turn over your top card. The player with the highest card, regardless of suit, wins the cards and puts them face-down at the bottom of his stack of cards. Ace is high and six is low, but if an ace and a six battle each other, the six wins. If the two cards tie in value, each player turns over another card face up. The player with the highest new cards wins all of the cards played, or, if there is another tie, the process is repeated.

Play continues until one player has all of the cards. In one version, that player is the drunkard because he has "all of the booze" and loses. In another version, the player who lost all of his cards is the drunkard because he "spent all his money" and loses the game!

A variation on play is if the cards tie one another. In this case, you each should place one card face down on the cards, and then one card face up. Either way of playing is acceptable but must be agreed on before play.

ALERT!

Scopone Scientifico (Italy)

Scopone Scientifico is an Italian game typically played with a forty-card Italian deck with suits of coins, cups, swords, and batons. The cards in that deck are one to seven and three suit cards. You can use your deck of fifty-two cards with the standard four suits—just remove the eight, nine, and ten of each suit. Scopone Scientifico is played with four players forming two teams, with partners sitting across from each other. The objective of the game is to capture cards of any suit from the table in an attempt to get as many points as possible.

Rules of Play

A random dealer is selected and deals a group of three cards to each player, another group of three cards to each player, and a final group of four cards to each player, all face down. Deal passes to the right with each hand.

ALERT!

You are not forced to capture any cards if you hold a card in your hand that is able to. However, if you play a card on the table that is able to make a capture, you must do so. You cannot just lay down the card and leave it on the table to capture at a later point.

Play begins with the player to the right of the dealer laying down a card from his hand to the table. He plays this card face up so everyone can view it. If the player to his right has a card of the same value, he may "capture" that card by laying down his card and picking up both his card and the first player's card. Otherwise, he lays down a second card to the table. Play continues around the table. When it's your turn, you must either lay down a card to the table or capture one or more cards. You can capture multiple cards by laying down a card with a value equal to the sum of two or more cards on the table. For example, you can lay down a nine and capture a five and a four, or a four, a three, and a two. The exception to this is that if you lay down a nine and there is a nine on the table, you must capture that single card. For the purposes of this game, the king is ranked as ten, the queen is nine, the jack is eight, and the seven through ace rank as seven through one.

When you capture cards, you must take the card that you laid down, plus the cards you captured, and lay them face down in a pile in front of you. If there are any cards remaining when the last card is played, the last player to pick up cards gets to pick up all cards on the table as a bonus.

Scoring the Hand

If you are able to clear all of the cards on the table with one card (a sweep), you score one point for "scopa." At the end of the game, four more points are determined. If your team captured the most cards during play, you win one point. If your team captured the most diamonds (coins) during play, you win one point. If your team captured the 7♦—the "sette bello"—during play, you win one point. If your team captured the best primiera, you win one point. The primiera is made up of your team's four highest valued cards, one in each suit. For the purpose of calculating scores in Scopone Scientifico, use these values:

- Sevens are worth twenty-one points
- Sixes are worth eighteen points
- Aces are worth sixteen points
- Fives are worth fifteen points
- Fours are worth fourteen points
- Threes are worth thirteen points
- Twos are worth twelve points
- Court cards (king, queen, and jack) are worth ten points

You'll notice that although the sevens aren't the highest-ranking cards for capturing other cards, they are the highest value in points. If you capture the 7♦, you're in really good shape!

All suits must be represented. If you do not have a card in each suit, your opponents automatically win the point for primiera. If both teams have a card in each suit, you compare the total of your highest four cards, and the team with the higher total wins the point. The first team to score eleven or more points at the end of a hand wins the game.

Zheng Fen (China)

Zheng Fen is a popular Chinese climbing and trick-taking game played with three to six players. The objective is to be the first player to score 500 points by taking tricks. Fives are worth five points, tens and kings are worth ten points, and the remaining cards are worth zero points. A standard deck of fifty-two cards is used, plus two jokers that have values of high and low. The cards rank from high to low as high joker, low joker, two, ace, king, queen, jack, ten, nine, eight, seven, six, five, four, and three. Suits are irrelevant.

Leading the First Trick

A random dealer is selected who deals out the entire deck, counterclockwise, to the players. Play begins with the dealer and continues counterclockwise. The player who holds the 3♥ leads the first trick. If you are that player, you have the option of playing one or more cards in a combination as follows:

- Any single card
- Pair of cards (pair)
- Three of a kind (triple)
- Four of a kind (quartet)
- Sequence of pairs—three or more pairs in an unbroken sequence, like 3 3 4 4 5 5
- Sequence of triples
- Sequence of quartets
- Full house—can consist of three of a kind and a pair, three of a kind and two cards in sequence of the same suit, three of a kind and a three and any other card, or three of a kind and two counting cards (five, ten, or king)

- Suit sequence—five or more cards in an unbroken sequence in one suit
- Special combinations—these combinations rank in order from low to high as follows: five, ten, and king in mixed suits; five, ten, and king in one suit; or four twos.

In any but the last three combinations, either of the jokers may be used to replace a natural card.

Beating a Trick

The next player must either pass or play a card or set of cards containing the same number of cards and matching the same pattern that the first player led. The cards he lays down must also beat the previous play. Any higher single card beats the previous single card. A group of cards is beaten by a higher-value group of the same number of cards. A full house is beaten by a higher-value three-of-a-kind. A sequence of cards is beaten by a higher-value sequence. You may also play a special combination, and that will beat the highest combination of cards played to that point. It is not necessary to beat the previous play just because you can. You can always pass and re-enter the round if you want.

Play continues around the table (multiple times if necessary) until a player lays down one or more cards and everyone else passes. All the cards played are then turned face down and placed to the side for the player who laid down cards last. That player starts again by laying down any single card, group of cards, or sequence of cards as described above. If a player whose turn it is to play has no more cards in his hand, the turn passes to the next counterclockwise player. Play continues until only one player holds cards in his hand. That player gives any points scored in his hand to the player who first went out. Each player counts the points in her hand (fives, tens, and kings) and adds that number to any previous score. The first player to go out of cards becomes the dealer of the next hand. He also leads the first trick of the next hand. The first player to go above 500 points (or 1,000 points, if you prefer a longer game) wins.

Chapter 20

Where to Play Games

You can always play cards with friends and family at your house, while camping, or even on an airplane. But there are other options as well. If you're up to trying a casino, you can play many of the gambling games. You can also play card games on the Internet or even in card groups. Here you'll learn the ins and outs of playing card games in various places.

Playing Blackjack at a Casino

Up to eight players can play at a blackjack table in a casino. The table is semicircular, and there is enough room for you to sit and keep your chips. The surface of the table is green felt. There is a circular area marked where you place your bet and a rectangular area where the dealer will place your cards. It's imperative that you check the table rules when you sit down to play. The table face itself will disclose the payout for blackjack and insurance bets and whether the dealer has to stand on seventeen. Somewhere on the table there will also be a notice of the minimum and maximum bet that can be placed. Many casinos also have specific rules on doubling down, splitting, dealing cards, and side bets. Ask the dealer about specific rules.

Dealer Hands

Don't be surprised if the dealer hits your hand or moves on without your signaling that you want to stand. When it's an obvious play, the dealer will sometimes automatically do it for you to speed up the game. Obvious plays include standing on a count of twenty or hitting on a count of six.

Although the dealer must stand on a count of seventeen, sometimes he is required to hit a soft seventeen (when he has a six and an ace).

Player Hands

Some casinos consider any ten and face card to be a pair and allow you to split them (although basic strategy suggests that you never split tens). You are also allowed to split again if you receive a pair in your first split. There is also an option to double down after you split a pair and are playing each hand. Most casinos only allow you to receive one card on each hand after splitting aces.

Some European casinos only allow you to take an insurance bet if you have a blackjack.

When it comes to doubling down, sometimes you can double down if your hand contains an ace, but sometimes you can only double down if your hand does not contain an ace.

Side Bets

There are often side bets allowed on the table. One of these bets is over/under thirteen, which is a bet that a player's first two cards will be greater or less than thirteen. Another bet is red/black, which is a side bet that the dealer's up card will be red or black. You can also place a bet that your first two cards will be of the same rank. Another bonus is when you are dealt three sevens, a six-seven-eight, or a king and queen of the same suit.

ALERT!

Side bets typically have a very high house edge—meaning more often than not, the casino will win. Experts normally advise you to stay clear of them. But if you're looking for a fun way to attempt to make additional money, go ahead and make a side bet or two.

Casino Video Poker

Video poker is an exciting game that combines the large payouts of slot machines with the skill of draw poker. The first video poker games were introduced in the 1970s with the advent of the computer chip, and the Jacks or Better machine was the earliest version to be played. The objective of video poker is the same as standard poker; that is, to win money by making the best possible poker hand. The only difference is that you're playing against a computer, so there's no need to bluff or fold a hand because you're afraid of losing too much money!

The majority of video poker games are variations on five-card draw. You are "dealt" five cards on the machine, and you choose which cards to discard and hold. The machine replaces the cards you discarded and pays out an amount based on your final hand. All video poker machines have the payout schedule listed on them that show how much you will be paid based on how many coins you inserted into the machine. You can usually insert up to five coins of the coin value listed on the machine, and you should always insert the maximum in order to take advantage of the bonuses. Hitting a royal flush pays a bonus if you've played the maximum number of coins.

Minimum Hands

There are different minimum hands required for payout in the video poker machines. In a Jack or Better machine, you must hold a pair of jacks at a minimum. A pair of tens or less causes you to lose your bet. On a Deuces Wild machine, all of the twos are wild cards. The minimum hand that pays out at this machine is a three-of-a-kind. A Joker's Wild machine includes a joker as a wild card. The minimum hand that pays out at this machine is two pair.

Video Poker Payouts

Even though video poker machines all are played basically the same way, various machines will pay out differently for different hands. A nine/seven machine means that you will be paid nine coins for a full house and seven coins for a flush. A seven/five or six/five machine gives the house a higher edge because you win fewer coins on hands smaller than a royal flush. Look for the machine that has the highest payout schedule. The progressive machines typically have lower payouts for the full house and the flush, but you might want to play them if the jackpot is high enough.

Video Poker Strategy

Expert players of video poker have come up with a strategy for drawing cards to improve your chances of winning money. If you have a four-of-a-kind or better, a full house, a flush, or a straight, keep all of your cards. If you have four cards that help to build a royal flush, a straight flush, a straight, or a flush, draw one card. If you have two pair, draw one card (although if you're playing Deuces Wild and the minimum hand is three-of-a-kind, you'll want to discard one pair and draw three cards). If you have a three-of-a-kind or three cards to a royal flush or a straight flush, draw two cards. If you have a pair, keep it and draw three cards. If you have two high cards, keep them and draw three cards. If you hold one high card, keep it and draw four cards. If you have nothing in your hand, discard them all and draw five cards. Some of the strategies vary depending on whether or not you are playing on a machine with wild cards.

Casino Poker Tables

Playing poker at a casino poker table can be a very daunting, albeit very exciting, way of gambling. Choosing the game you want to play should be relatively easy. Make sure to pick a game that you're familiar with. The games you will most often see include Texas Hold 'Em, Omaha Hold 'Em, and seven-card stud. You will never see variations like Anaconda or Follow the Queen in a casino. Card rooms never use wild cards except for the joker. When you enter the poker room, you will need to sign in at the desk and tell the host what game you are interested in playing. If there is an immediate opening, they will seat you. Otherwise they will put you on a waiting list until a seat is available.

Before you sit down at a table, you'll need to purchase chips. Poker games are typically played "table stakes," meaning that you can only bet the chips you have on the table. If you run out, you can't pull out more cash and buy more in the middle of a hand. If you run out of chips during the middle of a hand, you must announce to the table that you are "all in." Any further bets from your opponents will be placed as side bets, and you will be ineligible to win them. You also won't participate in any further betting rounds, you just continue to collect cards or discard cards until the play is over.

If you're playing a game with blinds, some casinos will require you to post the big blind immediately to join in, or to sit out the game until the big blind comes to your seat. When it's your turn to bet, place the chips in front of you instead of throwing them into the middle of the table. If you're making a raise, place the call bet and the money you're raising in front of you in one stack. You are not allowed to make "string bets," in which you place the money to call the bet on the table and then reach back to your chips for more money to raise. (To avoid this, you can also say "Raise" as soon as you put money down—that way there is no confusion.)

Card Groups

Playing in a card group can be a great way to socialize, meet with friends, and enjoy some healthy competition. You can find card groups for canasta, euchre, whist, bridge, hearts, spades, pinochle, poker, rummy, skat, cribbage, 500, and just about any game you like to play. These groups meet as often as once a week or once a month in places like church rooms, community centers, or even in the player's homes. In games that require partners, you can either keep your own partner or rotate partners throughout the year. Often card groups host tournaments within the group as well.

Join a Group

Depending on where you live and what games are popular in your area, there may be more than one group for the game that you prefer. You can call your local community center, YMCA, church, synagogue, or even check your local paper.

If you have access to the Internet, check out the Web site ✍ *www.meetup.com* to search for card game groups in your area.

Once you find a location, check out the time and days of play. Some groups meet on weekend mornings, while others meet on weekday evenings. Many of the groups offer food and drinks, but you may be charged a small fee. You'll also want to find out about the level at which the current players play. If you're new to the game and want instructional or basic play, that will be a different group from players who have been playing for years and want fast and strategic play. If you're going to be heading out to a poker night, make sure you know the minimum bet and take enough money to play!

Starting a Group

Just as with joining any group, there are a few steps you need to follow before setting up a new card group. First, choose a card game to be your focus, or decide that you will all rotate through various card games each time you meet. Next, you'll want to establish a location, frequency of get-togethers, day of the week, and time of day that your group will meet. If the location requires a fee for the room, or if you want to serve food, you may want to charge a small fee to the members of your group. If you're playing at someone's house, you may want to ask your group members to bring some food or drinks for a potluck. Finally, you'll want to advertise your group. You can do this by putting out flyers, contacting your friends and family, putting out an advertisement on bulletin boards or in the paper, or even setting up a Web site containing the information.

Online Gaming

If it's 2:00 in the morning and you're looking for a bridge card partner, or you want to play a quick game of blackjack, online gaming is definitely for you. Online casinos and card game forums have taken the world by storm. You can choose to play card games in virtual card rooms for free, download games to your personal computer to play by yourself, or gamble using real money at the online casinos.

Virtual Card Rooms

There are many Web sites that provide virtual card rooms for you to play games against live people elsewhere in the world. Check out Appendix B for a list of some popular Web sites. To log onto the Web site, you'll first create an account. You'll give your name, some demographic information, and then you can pick a username (nickname) and password. Some sites even allow you to pick a graphic image to represent you during play.

After you create an account, you can then pick the card game you wish to play by scrolling through a list of games. You click on the game you want and then have the option of picking your room and type of play: beginner, intermediate, expert, social, competitive, instructional, or some other variation of these. Within each room are various playing tables. Empty spots and tables will be clearly noted. You can choose to watch a game in process or actually "sit" down at a table and play. When you choose a table, a new screen will appear that is just your table. You will see the other players on the table, your card hand, buttons for playing (the buttons will vary based on the game you chose), and typically an area for chatting with the other players.

The dealer at online casinos is actually a random number generator (RNG). Most casinos use sophisticated RNGs that have been tested by running millions of game scenarios that are reviewed for their accuracy.

ALERT!

Don't give out too much information, especially personal information, in the chat, as anybody can see it. You should never get so involved with chatting that you hold up the game and don't pay attention to your cards.

Downloading Games

The majority of card games have Web sites that allow you to download shareware (free) programs, or software for a price, so that you can play the game on your personal computer. Once you have downloaded and installed the software, you can launch the game and play solitaire games or play other card games against the computer. Most games have various options of play, and they usually include an explanation of the rules or instructions, in case you're unsure of what to do.

Online Casinos

If you're looking to play with money on the Internet, online casinos are for you. When looking for a Web site where you can play, you need to check out their frequently asked questions (FAQ) or "about us" section and make sure that they are properly owned, licensed, bonded, have the proper insurance, and are approved by a gaming commission. Casinos based in countries such as Antigua, Costa Rica, the West Indies, and Australia are recommended. You also need to verify that your payment information is secure and that your personal information will not be sold to a third party. Check for a toll-free number and customer support before entering any information. You must be eighteen years or older and have a valid credit card to play. Make sure that you learn the casino's payout rules and check for any hidden fees that the casino charges.

As with any gambling, set a budget and stick to it. Only gamble with money that you can afford to lose. Don't go into debt by gambling money you don't have. Don't play if you under the influence of drugs or alcohol or even if you are upset about something. You need to be clear-headed and focused when it comes to gambling with real money. Expect to lose, and if you win, take your money and log off for the day!

Appendices

Appendix A

Glossary

Appendix B

Resources and Web Sites

Appendix A

Glossary

21:
The winning total in blackjack, or another name for the game.

ABOVE THE LINE:
Points that do not count toward the game (bridge) and that are placed above the line on the scoring sheet.

ACT:
To do something when it's your turn.

ACTION:
The amount of money a player wagers.

ADVERSARY:
Any opponent or someone playing against the high bidder.

ALONE:
In euchre, when a player chooses not to play with his partner.

ANTE:
A small portion of the minimum bet that each player is required to put into the pot before a new hand can start.

AROUND:
A set of four aces, kings, queens, or jacks of all different suits.

ARTIFICIAL BID:
A bid with a special meaning unrelated to the suit bid.

ASSIST:
In euchre, when the dealer's partner agrees to keep the up card as trump.

AUCTION:
A period of bidding before the cards are played.

AVAILABLE:
In solitaire, a card that is not blocked and may be moved elsewhere on the table.

BACK DOOR:
In bezique, a sequence in a plain suit.

BACK HAND:
In Pai Gow or Chinese Poker, the top five-card hand.

BACK IN:
Coming back into the round of betting after previously checking or passing.

BALANCED HAND:
A hand of cards with no voids or single cards in a suit.

BANK:
The dealer in a gambling game.

BANKER:
The dealer whom all players play against.

BANKROLL:
The available money the player plans to bet with.

BASIC STRATEGY:
A computer-developed method for playing blackjack that is easily memorized by a player without counting cards.

BEG:
In All Fours, the player on the dealer's left proposes to the dealer to deal out three additional cards to each player and turn up a new trump suit.

BELOW THE LINE:
Points that count toward the game (bridge) and that are placed below the line on the scoring sheet.

BEST:
Highest ranking.

BEST BOWER:
The joker as the highest trump.

BET:
Wager.

BETTING LIMITS:
The minimum and maximum amounts of money that a player can wager on one bet.

BID:
An agreement to win at least the number of tricks indicated by the bid (with a partner or solo).

BIDDER:
The person who makes a bid.

BIG JOKER:
The higher of two jokers.

BLACKJACK:
A ten or face card and an ace, as first two cards a player is dealt.

BLACK THREE:
The 3♠ or 3♣. In canasta, these are safe discards and cannot be melded.

BLACK WIDOW:
Queen of spades.

BLIND:
A forced bet (or partial bet) put in by one or more players before any cards are dealt.

BLITZ:
In gin rummy, winning against an opponent who has failed to score.

BLOCK:
A player or all players are unable to play.

BLUFF:
A play or bid that is deceptive.

BOARD:
In poker, the community cards dealt face-up in the center of the table.

BOODLE CARD:
Extra cards from a second deck where players place their ante.

BOOK:
The first six tricks taken by the declarer.

BOWER:
In euchre, the jack of a suit.

BREAK:
Laying the first card or meld.

BREAK-EVEN HAND:
The hand at which a player's losses equal winnings.

BREAKING HAND (STIFF):
A hand that could break (go over twenty-one) with a one-card draw, such as a hard twelve, thirteen, fourteen, fifteen, or sixteen.

BUILD:
In solitaire, transfer cards around the table.

BUMP:
To raise.

BURN:
To discard the top card from the deck, face down, so that any player cannot see the next card.

BUST:
In blackjack, when the dealer or player goes over twenty-one.

CALL:
In poker, when a player matches the current bet on the table. In keno and bingo, to draw the numbers for each game.

CANASTA:
A meld of seven or more matching cards.

CAP:
To put in the last raise permitted on a betting round.

CAPTURE:
To win a trick.

CARD COUNTING:
When a player keeps track of all the cards that have been played.

CASE:
The last card of a specific rank in the deck.

CHECK:
To not bet, with the option to call or raise later.

CHIPS:
Round tokens used to represent cash.

CLUBS:
The suit denoted by ♣.

COLD:
A player who is on a losing streak.

COMBINED HAND:
The cards making up both hands of the team.

COMMON MARRIAGE:
A queen and king of the same nontrump suit.

COMPLETE HAND:
A poker hand that uses all five cards, such as a straight, flush, full house, four-of-a-kind, or straight flush.

CONCEDE:
To give up your hand to the opponent.

CONTRACT:
A bet that a player will take a certain amount of tricks.

COPY:
In Pai Gow, a player and the banker have the same two-card hand or five-card hand.

COUNT:
The value of a hand.

COURT CARDS:
The king, queen, and jack.

COVER:
To play a higher card than the card led.

CRAWL:
To play a higher-ranking card in the suit led.

CRIB:
In cribbage, an extra hand for the dealer, formed by the players' discards.

CUT:
To divide the deck. The cards are then placed back together and dealt.

CUT-THROAT:
Each player plays independently instead of in teams.

DEADWOOD:
In gin rummy, cards held in a hand that cannot be melded.

DEAL:
To give out the cards to the players.

DEALER:
The person who deals the cards.

DECLARATION:
Call, bid, or naming of trump.

DECLARER:
The player who bid the last contract in bridge. It's this person's responsibility to win the number of tricks bid.

DEFENDERS:
The opponents of the declarer.

DEUCE:
Two of any suit.

DIAMONDS:
The suit denoted by ♦.

DISCARD:
To play a card that is not of the suit led or of the trump suit.

DOUBLE DOWN:
The player's option to turn her two cards face-up and double her original bet to get one additional card.

DOUBLE SKUNK:
In cribbage, a bonus for the winner if he beats his opponent by sixty-one or more points.

DOUBLETON:
Two cards in a suit.

DRAW:
To obtain additional cards. In draw poker, it's the second round of cards that are dealt.

DUMMY:
The declarer's partner.

EDGE:
An advantage over one's opponent.

EQUITY:
A player's share of a pot.

EUCHRE:
In euchre, a failure to win three tricks.

FACE CARD:
The king, queen, or jack of any suit of cards.

FIFTEEN:
In cribbage, playing a card that brings the total to fifteen, earning the player two points.

FIFTH STREET:
In seven-card stud poker, the third round of betting. In Hold 'Em, the fifth card on board and the final round of betting.

FIRST BASE:
The first seat at the blackjack table, immediately to the left of the dealer.

FLAT BET:
A bet that the player does not vary.

FLOP:
In Hold 'Em, the three cards dealt face up in the center of the table.

FLUSH:
Five cards of the same suit.

FOLD:
A player drops out of the hand.

FOLLOW SUIT:
Playing a card of the suit that was led.

FORCE:
Forcing someone to play a trump to take the lead.

FOUR OF A KIND:
Four cards of the same value.

FROZEN:
A discard pile that cannot be taken without a natural pair in one's hand.

FULL HOUSE:
A three-of-a-kind and a pair.

GIN:
In gin rummy, when all the cards in the hand are melded.

GO:
In cribbage, to signify that a player cannot play another card without going over thirty-one.

GOING OUT:
Getting rid of all the cards in a player's hand.

GRAND SLAM:
Requires the declarer to win all thirteen tricks.

HAND:
The cards dealt to a player. Also, the play that happens in between deals.

HARD COUNT:
The true face value of the cards being played with.

HARD HAND:
A hand without an ace, or a hand with an ace that can only be counted as a one to avoid going over twenty-one.

HEARTS:
The suit denoted by ♥.

HEEL:
A jack starter card.

HIGH ROLLER:
A big better.

HIT:
To take another card.

HOLE CARD:
In blackjack, the dealer's face down card. In stud

and Hold 'Em poker, the face-down cards dealt to each player.

HONORS:
The royalty of bridge: ace, king, queen, jack, and ten.

HOT:
A player who is on a winning streak.

HUITIÈME:
In piquet, a sequence of eight cards scoring eighteen points.

INSURANCE:
Side wager for up to half of the original wager when the dealer is showing an ace.

JACK:
In All Fours, one point scored for winning the jack of trumps.

JOKER:
An extra card added to the standard deck of fifty-two cards. Often used as a wild card.

KITTY:
Crib.

KNAVE:
Jack.

LAY OFF:
In rummy, to get rid of your cards by playing on your opponent's melds.

LEAD:
The first card played in a trick.

LEFT BOWER:
In euchre, the jack of the same color as the

jack of the trump suit.

LEG:
One length of the cribbage board (thirty holes).

LITTLE JOKER:
The lower ranking of two jokers.

LONG SUIT:
Holding more than four cards in one suit.

MAJORS:
The top two suits in bridge for bidding—spades and hearts.

MARRIAGE:
A king and queen of the same suit.

MELD:
A combination of three cards having a value in scoring.

MIDDLEHAND:
In skat, the player to the dealer's right.

MINORS:
The bottom two suits in bridge for bidding—diamonds and clubs.

MISERE:
In Solo Whist, a contract not to win a trick.

MUGGINS:
In cribbage, taking an opponent's points that he overlooked.

NATURAL:
In blackjack, a two-card hand that equals twenty-one points (a ten or face card and an ace). Pays winner 3:2. In canasta, a nonwild card.

NIL:
A bid by a player trying not to take tricks.

NOB:
A jack of the same suit as the starter card.

NULL:
A contract to take no tricks.

OPEN:
The player who bets first.

OVERTRICK:
Each trick won in excess of the contract.

PAIR:
Two cards of the same value.

PARTNER:
Two players who act as a team.

PASS:
To not bet.

PAT HAND:
In blackjack, a hand with a total of seventeen to twenty-one. In draw poker, a hand that does not need any more cards.

PEDRO:
In Cinch, the five of trumps or the five of the same color suit as trumps.

PEG:
In cribbage, a marker used for scoring.

PENALTY:
Bonuses awarded to the defenders.

PINOCHLE:
A meld of the Q♠ and J♦.

PIP VALUE:
The numerical value of a card.

PIT BOSS:
The person at a casino who is in charge of the games.

PITCH:
In Auction Pitch, the opening lead that declares the trump suit.

POINT:
A unit of scoring.

POINT COUNT:
The net value of the card count at the end of a hand.

POT:
The amount of chips or money at stake.

PRESS:
To increase the amount being wagered after a win, usually by the original amount.

PUSH:
A tie between the player and the dealer. No winner or loser.

QUART:
In piquet, a sequence of four cards scoring four points.

QUATORZE:
In piquet, four aces, kings, queens, jacks, or tens scoring fourteen points.

QUINT:
In piquet, a sequence of five cards scoring five points.

RAISE:
A player matches the previous bet and then bets more.

RANK:
A card's hierarchy.

RED THREE:
A 3♥ or 3♦. In canasta, these score bonus points.

REVOKE:
A failure to follow suit when able or not playing within the rules of the game.

RIGHT BOWER:
In euchre, the jack of the trump suit.

RIVER:
The final card dealt in a hand of stud or Hold 'Em. In seven-card stud, a player who stays in until the fifth round of betting is said to be "going to the river."

ROUNDHOUSE:
A marriage in every suit.

ROYAL FLUSH:
An ace-high straight flush.

ROYAL MARRIAGE:
A queen and king of the trump suit.

RUBBER:
In bridge, a series of three games won by the person who wins the majority (two).

RUN:
A sequence of three or more cards in the same suit.

SCHNEIDER:
A hand in which one side takes at least ninety-one points.

SCHWARZ:
A hand in which one side takes all the tricks.

SEPTIÈME:
In piquet, a sequence of seven cards scoring seventeen points.

SHOE:
A rectangular dealing device.

SHUFFLE:
To mix the cards up at random.

SIDE SUIT:
A suit other than the trump suit.

SINGLETON:
A single card in one suit in a hand.

SIXIÈME:
In piquet, a sequence of six cards scoring sixteen points.

SKUNK:
To win in cribbage when the player has not yet reached the last leg of the board.

SOFT HAND:
A hand that uses the ace as an eleven.

SPADES:
The suit denoted by ♠.

SPLIT:
The player has two cards of the same value and splits those cards to play each hand individually.

STAND:
To not draw anymore cards.

STIFF HAND:
A hand between twelve and sixteen.

STARTER:
The up card when the deck is cut.

STRAIGHT:
Five cards of consecutive values.

STRAIGHT FLUSH:
Five cards of consecutive values within the same suit.

SURRENDER:
When the player discards his hand and gives up half of his bet. Must be done before any cards are drawn.

THIRD BASE:
The last seat at the blackjack table, immediately to the right of the dealer.

THIRD STREET:
In seven-card stud, the first round of betting.

THREE OF A KIND:
Three cards of the same value.

TIERCE:
In piquet, a sequence of three cards scoring three points.

TOKE:
The tip or gratuity given to a dealer.

TREY:
A three of any suit.

TRICK:
Each player plays a card and the highest card of the suit led (or trump) wins. Those four cards are called a trick and are taken by the player who won.

TRIO:
In piquet, three aces, kings, queens, or jacks scoring three points.

TRUMP:
A suit of cards chosen at random or through bidding.

UNDERTRICK:
Each trick short of a player's original bid.

UP CARD:
The dealer's face-up card.

VOID:
No cards in a particular suit in a hand.

WILD CARD:
A joker or other card that can substitute for a card needed in a player's hand.

Appendix B

Resources and Web Sites

Organizations, Associations, and Clubs

American Bridge Association
2828 Lakewood Ave. SW
Atlanta, GA 30315
Phone: 404-768-5517
✐ www.americanbridge.com

American Bridge Teachers' Association
14840 Crystal Cove Court, #503
Fort Myers, FL 33919-7417
Phone: 239-437-4106
✐ www.abtahome.com

American Contract Bridge League
2990 Airways Blvd.
Memphis, TN 38116-3847
Phone: 800-467-1623
✐ www.acbl.org

American Cribbage Congress
Find local clubs and Internet cribbage sites.
✐ www.cribbage.org

Bid Whist Clubs
✐ www.sharksinc.com

Canadian Bridge Federation
2719 East Jolly Place
Regina SK S4V 0X8
Phone: 306-761-1677
✐ www.cbf.ca

Euchre Club
✐ www.come.to/euchre

The Euchre Exchange (Yahoo Clubs)
✐ http://groups.yahoo.com/group/theeuchreexchange

International Skat Players Association
✐ http://ispaworld.org

Iplay—Find local clubs and leagues
✐ http://clubs.iplay.net

Meetup—Find card groups in your area for the game you're interested in.
✐ www.meetup.com

National Pinochle Association
✐ http://members.aol.com/ampinochle/npa/index.html

Okbridge—Play bridge online and in tournaments with people across the globe.
✐ www.okbridge.com

Power Players Pinochle—Find out or list your own pinochle event information.
✐ http://pinochle.webappeal.com

The Sheepshead Association
✐ www.sheepshead.org

Tournament of Players—Play in hearts tournaments.
✍ *www.toptourney.com*

United States Bridge Federation
2990 Airways Blvd.
Memphis, TN 38116-3847
Phone: 901-332-5586, ext. 307
✍ *www.usbf.org*

World Bridge Federation
✍ *www.worldbridge.org*

World Poker Tour
✍ *www.worldpokertour.com*

Further Learning and Tips

Absolute Gin Rummy
Learn about the history, deal, variations, strategy, and tips for playing gin rummy.
✍ *www.absoluteginrummy.com*

Free Blackjack Tips
Learn the rules, strategy, betting systems, card counting, and more.
✍ *www.freeblackjacktips.com*

John McLeod's Card Games Web Site
A wealth of information for card games from all parts of the world.
✍ *www.pagat.com*

Learn That
Learn how to play hearts, euchre, and spades.
✍ *www.learnthat.com*

PokerTips
Poker strategy for beginner, intermediate, and advanced players.
✍ *www.pokertips.org*

The Rules of the Game
Instructions for poker, hearts, Crazy Eights, blackjack, bridge, and whist.
✍ *www.webterrACE.com/cards/home.htm*

Further Reading

The Bridge World (magazine)
✍ *www.bridgeworld.com*

The Bridge Companion (magazine)
✍ *www.bridgecompanion.com*

Andrews, Joseph. *Win at Hearts*. (Bonus Books, 2000).

Barlow, Dan. *Play Cribbage to Win*. (Sterling, 2000).

Brown, Douglas. *150 Solitaire Games*. (Harper-Resource, 1991).

Bumppo, Natty. *The Columbus Book of Euchre*. (Borf Books, 1999).

Buttler, Frank and Simon. *Spades for Winners*. (Master Spades, 2001).

Ellis, John. *Euchre: The Grandpa Lou Way*. (Bayeux Arts, Inc. 1997).

Fleishman, Steve. *Cribbage*. (Trafalgar Square, 2000).

Fry, Sam. *Gin Rummy: How to Play and Win.* (Dover Pubns., 1978).

Hervey, George and Parlett, David. *Card Games for One.* (McGraw Hill, 1994).

Jacoby, Oswald. *How to Win at Gin Rummy.* (Henry Holt & Company, Inc., 1978).

Killebrew, Charlie. *Play Gin to Win.* (Charles F. Killebrew, 1999).

Phillips, Larry W. *The Tao of Poker: 285 Rules to Transform Your Game and Your Life.* (Adams Media Corporation, 2003).

Reese, Terence. *Bridge for Bright Beginners.* (Dover Pubns., 1973).

Root, William S. *The ABCs of Bridge.* (Three River Press, 1998).

Sklansky, David. *Hold 'Em Poker.* (Two Plus Two Publishing LLC, 1996).

Sklansky, David. *The Theory of Poker.* (Two Plus Two Publishing LLC, 1999).

Truscott, Alan. *Basic Bridge in Three Weeks.* (Perigree, 1987).

Vancura, Olaf and Fuchs, Ken. *Knock-Out Blackjack: The Easiest Card-Counting System Ever.* (Huntington Press, 1998).

Wong, Stanford. *Professional Blackjack.* (Pi Yee Press, 2004).

Download Card Games for Your Computer

Advanced Video Poker
Download and play seven variations of video poker games.
www.aimgames.com

Free Spades
Download spades, hearts, euchre, gin, or cribbage (free).
http://freespades.com

igrecs
Download video poker (free).
http://igrecs.com

Online Casinos Strategy Guide
Download Pai Gow
www.online-casinos-strategy.com

Download Caribbean Stud Poker
www.online-casinos-strategy.com

Shareup
Download Scopone Scientifico ($25)
www.shareup.net

Simtel
Download various card games
www.simtel.net

SmartBridge
Download bridge (free).
http://smartbridge.netfirms.com/index.htm

The Nelsons Domain
Download Brag (free).
www.nelsonsdomain.co.uk/brag.html

Play Card Games Online

e-bridge
The largest bridge tournament club.
✎ *www.e-bridgemaster.com*

Game Colony
Play online poker, Free Cell, solitaire, gin rummy, and cribbage.
✎ *www.gamecolony.com*

Games.com
Play Klondike solitaire, Pyramid solitaire, blackjack, bridge, cribbage, euchre, gin, hearts, or spades.
✎ *http://play.games.com/playgames/home.jsp*

Iplay
Play canasta, cribbage, euchre, gin rummy, hearts, pinochle, spades, and more.
✎ *http://clubs.iplay.net*

MSN.com
Play bridge, cribbage, euchre, hearts, spades, and solitaire.
✎ *http://zone.msn.com/en/root/cardandboard.htm*

OKbridge
Play bridge online and in tournaments with people across the globe.
✎ *www.okbridge.com*

Playcards.net
Play cyber spades with others online.
✎ *www.playcards.net*

Pogo.com
Play bridge, cribbage, euchre, solitaire, hearts, Free Cell, and spades.
✎ *www.pogo.com*

Yahoo Games
Play online games such as solitaire, blackjack, bridge, canasta, cribbage, Deuces Wild, euchre, Free Cell, gin, Go Fish, Golf, hearts, poker, pinochle, Pyramids, Sheepshead, and spades!
✎ *http://games.yahoo.com*

Online Casinos

Casino Tropez
✎ *www.casinotropez.com*

Delano Casino
✎ *www.delanocasino.com*

49er Casino
✎ *www.49ercasino.com/*

Golden Tiger
✎ *www.goldentigercasino.com*

InterCasino
✎ *www.intercasino.com*

Lucky Nugget
✎ *www.luckynugget.com*

Omni Casino
✎ *www.omnicasino.com*

PlanetLuck
✎ *www.planetluck.com*

Shark Casino
✎ *www.sharkcasino.com*

Online Casino Tips
Lots of helpful tips about online gaming, including a blacklist of unscrupulous sites.
✎ *www.online-casino-tips.com*

Index

Index

THE EVERYTHING SERIES!

BUSINESS

Everything® Business Planning Book
Everything® Coaching and Mentoring Book
Everything® Fundraising Book
Everything® Home-Based Business Book
Everything® Landlording Book
Everything® Leadership Book
Everything® Managing People Book
Everything® Negotiating Book
Everything® Network Marketing Book
Everything® Online Business Book
Everything® Project Management Book
Everything® Robert's Rules Book,
       $7.95($11.95 CAN)
Everything® Selling Book
Everything® Start Your Own Business Book
Everything® Time Management Book

COMPUTERS

Everything® Build Your Own Home Page Book
Everything® Computer Book

COOKBOOKS

Everything® Barbecue Cookbook
Everything® Bartender's Book, $9.95
       ($15.95 CAN)
Everything® Chinese Cookbook
Everything® Chocolate Cookbook
Everything® Cookbook
Everything® Dessert Cookbook
Everything® Diabetes Cookbook
Everything® Fondue Cookbook
Everything® Grilling Cookbook
Everything® Holiday Cookbook
Everything® Indian Cookbook
Everything® Low-Carb Cookbook
Everything® Low-Fat High-Flavor Cookbook
Everything® Low-Salt Cookbook
Everything® Mediterranean Cookbook
Everything® Mexican Cookbook
Everything® One-Pot Cookbook

Everything® Pasta Cookbook
Everything® Quick Meals Cookbook
Everything® Slow Cooker Cookbook
Everything® Soup Cookbook
Everything® Thai Cookbook
Everything® Vegetarian Cookbook
Everything® Wine Book

HEALTH

Everything® Alzheimer's Book
Everything® Anti-Aging Book
Everything® Diabetes Book
Everything® Dieting Book
Everything® Hypnosis Book
Everything® Low Cholesterol Book
Everything® Massage Book
Everything® Menopause Book
Everything® Nutrition Book
Everything® Reflexology Book
Everything® Reiki Book
Everything® Stress Management Book
Everything® Vitamins, Minerals, and
       Nutritional Supplements Book

HISTORY

Everything® American Government Book
Everything® American History Book
Everything® Civil War Book
Everything® Irish History & Heritage Book
Everything® Mafia Book
Everything® Middle East Book

HOBBIES & GAMES

Everything® Bridge Book
Everything® Candlemaking Book
Everything® Card Games Book
Everything® Cartooning Book
Everything® Casino Gambling Book, 2nd Ed.
Everything® Chess Basics Book
Everything® Collectibles Book
Everything® Crossword and Puzzle Book

Everything® Crossword Challenge Book
Everything® Drawing Book
Everything® Digital Photography Book
Everything® Easy Crosswords Book
Everything® Family Tree Book
Everything® Games Book
Everything® Knitting Book
Everything® Magic Book
Everything® Motorcycle Book
Everything® Online Genealogy Book
Everything® Photography Book
Everything® Poker Strategy Book
Everything® Pool & Billiards Book
Everything® Quilting Book
Everything® Scrapbooking Book
Everything® Sewing Book
Everything® Soapmaking Book

HOME IMPROVEMENT

Everything® Feng Shui Book
Everything® Feng Shui Decluttering Book,
       $9.95 ($15.95 CAN)
Everything® Fix-It Book
Everything® Homebuilding Book
Everything® Home Decorating Book
Everything® Landscaping Book
Everything® Lawn Care Book
Everything® Organize Your Home Book

EVERYTHING®
KIDS' BOOKS

All titles are $6.95 ($10.95 Canada)
unless otherwise noted
Everything® Kids' Baseball Book, 3rd Ed.
Everything® Kids' Bible Trivia Book
Everything® Kids' Bugs Book
Everything® Kids' Christmas Puzzle
       & Activity Book
Everything® Kids' Cookbook
Everything® Kids' Halloween Puzzle
       & Activity Book ($9.95 CAN)

All Everything® books are priced at $12.95 or $14.95, unless otherwise stated. Prices subject to change without notice.
Canadian prices range from $11.95–$31.95, and are subject to change without notice.

Everything® Kids' Hidden Pictures Book
($9.95 CAN)
Everything® Kids' Joke Book
Everything® Kids' Knock Knock Book
($9.95 CAN)
Everything® Kids' Math Puzzles Book
Everything® Kids' Mazes Book
Everything® Kids' Money Book ($11.95 CAN)
Everything® Kids' Monsters Book
Everything® Kids' Nature Book ($11.95 CAN)
Everything® Kids' Puzzle Book
Everything® Kids' Riddles & Brain Teasers Book
Everything® Kids' Science Experiments Book
Everything® Kids' Soccer Book
Everything® Kids' Travel Activity Book

KIDS' STORY BOOKS

Everything® Bedtime Story Book
Everything® Bible Stories Book
Everything® Fairy Tales Book
Everything® Mother Goose Book

LANGUAGE

Everything® Conversational Japanese Book
(with CD), $19.95 ($31.95 CAN)
Everything® Inglés Book
Everything® French Phrase Book, $9.95
($15.95 CAN)
Everything® Learning French Book
Everything® Learning German Book
Everything® Learning Italian Book
Everything® Learning Latin Book
Everything® Learning Spanish Book
Everything® Sign Language Book
Everything® Spanish Phrase Book,
$9.95 ($15.95 CAN)
Everything® Spanish Verb Book,
$9.95 ($15.95 CAN)

MUSIC

Everything® Drums Book (with CD),
$19.95 ($31.95 CAN)
Everything® Guitar Book
Everything® Home Recording Book
Everything® Playing Piano and Keyboards Book
Everything® Rock & Blues Guitar Book
(with CD), $19.95 ($31.95 CAN)
Everything® Songwriting Book

NEW AGE

Everything® Astrology Book
Everything® Divining the Future Book
Everything® Dreams Book
Everything® Ghost Book
Everything® Love Signs Book,
$9.95 ($15.95 CAN)
Everything® Meditation Book
Everything® Numerology Book
Everything® Paganism Book
Everything® Palmistry Book
Everything® Psychic Book
Everything® Spells & Charms Book
Everything® Tarot Book
Everything® Wicca and Witchcraft Book

PARENTING

Everything® Baby Names Book
Everything® Baby Shower Book
Everything® Baby's First Food Book
Everything® Baby's First Year Book
Everything® Birthing Book
Everything® Breastfeeding Book
Everything® Father-to-Be Book
Everything® Get Ready for Baby Book
Everything® Getting Pregnant Book
Everything® Homeschooling Book
Everything® Parent's Guide to Children
with Asperger's Syndrome
Everything® Parent's Guide to Children
with Autism
Everything® Parent's Guide to Children
with Dyslexia
Everything® Parent's Guide to Positive Discipline
Everything® Parent's Guide to Raising a
Successful Child
Everything® Parenting a Teenager Book
Everything® Potty Training Book,
$9.95 ($15.95 CAN)
Everything® Pregnancy Book, 2nd Ed.
Everything® Pregnancy Fitness Book
Everything® Pregnancy Nutrition Book
Everything® Pregnancy Organizer,
$15.00 ($22.95 CAN)
Everything® Toddler Book
Everything® Tween Book

PERSONAL FINANCE

Everything® Budgeting Book
Everything® Get Out of Debt Book

Everything® Get Rich Book
Everything® Homebuying Book, 2nd Ed.
Everything® Homeselling Book
Everything® Investing Book
Everything® Money Book
Everything® Mutual Funds Book
Everything® Online Business Book
Everything® Personal Finance Book
Everything® Personal Finance in Your
20s & 30s Book
Everything® Real Estate Investing Book
Everything® Wills & Estate Planning Book

PETS

Everything® Cat Book
Everything® Dog Book
Everything® Dog Training and Tricks Book
Everything® Golden Retriever Book
Everything® Horse Book
Everything® Labrador Retriever Book
Everything® Poodle Book
Everything® Puppy Book
Everything® Rottweiler Book
Everything® Tropical Fish Book

REFERENCE

Everything® Astronomy Book
Everything® Car Care Book
Everything® Christmas Book,
$15.00 ($21.95 CAN)
Everything® Classical Mythology Book
Everything® Einstein Book
Everything® Etiquette Book
Everything® Great Thinkers Book
Everything® Philosophy Book
Everything® Psychology Book
Everything® Shakespeare Book
Everything® Tall Tales, Legends, & Other
Outrageous Lies Book
Everything® Toasts Book
Everything® Trivia Book
Everything® Weather Book

RELIGION

Everything® Angels Book
Everything® Bible Book
Everything® Buddhism Book
Everything® Catholicism Book
Everything® Christianity Book
Everything® Jewish History & Heritage Book

All Everything® books are priced at $12.95 or $14.95, unless otherwise stated. Prices subject to change without notice.
Canadian prices range from $11.95–$31.95, and are subject to change without notice.

Everything® Judaism Book
Everything® Koran Book
Everything® Prayer Book
Everything® Saints Book
Everything® Understanding Islam Book
Everything® World's Religions Book
Everything® Zen Book

SCHOOL & CAREERS

Everything® After College Book
Everything® Alternative Careers Book
Everything® College Survival Book
Everything® Cover Letter Book
Everything® Get-a-Job Book
Everything® Hot Careers Book
Everything® Job Interview Book
Everything® New Teacher Book
Everything® Online Job Search Book
Everything® Personal Finance Book
Everything® Practice Interview Book
Everything® Resume Book, 2nd Ed.
Everything® Study Book

SELF-HELP/ RELATIONSHIPS

Everything® Dating Book
Everything® Divorce Book
Everything® Great Marriage Book
Everything® Great Sex Book
Everything® Kama Sutra Book
Everything® Romance Book
Everything® Self-Esteem Book
Everything® Success Book

SPORTS & FITNESS

Everything® Body Shaping Book
Everything® Fishing Book
Everything® Fly-Fishing Book
Everything® Golf Book
Everything® Golf Instruction Book
Everything® Knots Book
Everything® Pilates Book
Everything® Running Book
Everything® Sailing Book, 2nd Ed.
Everything® T'ai Chi and QiGong Book
Everything® Total Fitness Book
Everything® Weight Training Book
Everything® Yoga Book

TRAVEL

Everything® Family Guide to Hawaii
Everything® Family Guide to New York City, 2nd Ed.
Everything® Family Guide to Washington D.C., 2nd Ed.

ok, $9.95
($15.95 CAN)
Everything® Creative Wedding Ideas Book
Everything® Elopement Book, $9.95
($15.95 CAN)
Everything® Father of the Bride Book,
$9.95 ($15.95 CAN)
Everything® Groom Book, $9.95 ($15.95 CAN)
Everything® Jewish Wedding Book
Everything® Mother of the Bride Book,
$9.95 ($15.95)
Everything® Wedding Book, 3rd Ed.
Everything® Wedding Checklist,
$7.95 ($12.95 CAN)
Everything® Wedding Etiquette Book,
$7.95 ($12.95 CAN)
Everything® Wedding Organizer,
$15.00 ($22.95 CAN)
Everything® Wedding Shower Book,
$7.95 ($12.95 CAN)
Everything® Wedding Vows Book,
$7.95 ($12.95 CAN)
Everything® Weddings on a Budget Book,
9.95 ($15.95 CAN)

WRITING

eative Writing Book
ublished Book
mar and Style Book
t Writing Book
e to Writing a Novel
e to Writing Children's Books
nwriting Book
g Well Book

Introdu
craft

All titles are $14.95 ($22.95 CAN)

Everything® Crafts—Create Your Own Greeting Cards
1-59337-226-4
Everything® Crafts—Polymer Clay for Beginners
1-59337-230-2

Everything® Crafts—Rubberstamping Made Easy
1-59337-229-9
Everything® Crafts—Wedding Decorations and Keepsakes
1-59337-227-2

Available wherever books are sold!
To order, call 800-872-5627, or visit us at **www.everything.com**
Everything® and everything.com® are registered trademarks of F+W Publications, Inc.